THEOLOGICAL
THEMES OF
YOUTH MINISTRY

THEOLOGICAL THEMES OF YOUTH MINISTRY

William Myers

Introduction by David Ng

THE PILGRIM PRESS   NEW YORK

All Scripture quotations, unless otherwise indicated, are from the Revised Standard Version of the Bible, copyrighted 1946, 1952, © 1971, 1973, by the Division of Christian Education of the National Council of Churches of Christ in the United States of America, and are used by permission. Additional acknowledgement of permissions are found in the Notes, pages 101–106.

Library of Congress Cataloging-in-Publication Data

Myers, William, 1942–
    Theological themes of youth ministry.

    Bibliography
    1. Church work with youth.   2. Church year.
I. Title.
BV4447.M94   1987   259'.2   87-18493
ISBN 0–8298–0756–X

The Pilgrim Press, 132 West 31 Street, New York, NY 10001

For William Alfred Myers

Contents

vii

Introduction

David Ng

Any book on youth ministry that avoids the word
"success" in its title already has my gratitude. When a
book on youth ministry digs deeper into this verdant
field (for some, a jungle), beyond the practical, to un-
earth that which is personal, relational, communal, religious, and theological, that book is a treasure.
Theological Themes of Youth Ministry is for the church and
for each youth leader such a treasure.

This book is personal. Every idea and image offered
(and the book is rich with images) come from the life
and person of its author, who has experienced and
reflected upon the activities described and the theological rationales behind them. They ring true. Because they
are true, we who also seek to serve the youth of the
church not only can believe what is written but can

identify with the ideas and wish to try them. We will try these ideas not because Bill Myers was successful (he was, but that is never the point in this book) but because he is faithful. The author calls us to faithfulness in our ministry with youth and to youth ministry which is incarnational; this is the approach given to the author by experience and by grace. We find it within our imagination that we can receive God's gifts and be incarnations of God's love in a community which incarnates love and grace.

This book is directed to the adult leader as a person. You are spoken to with respect and with high expectations that you will use your imagination. The youth ministry described here is not an ornate stage set literally constructed and begging for imitation. The set has form—theological and liturgical—but on this stage youth ministry is sketched out, and you, as the viewer must supply your own perceptions and match your own experiences and insights with those of the author. The stage is carefully crafted but you must see for yourself. This is your personal book about youth ministry.

Many images are offered from biblical and other literary sources. Young people and leaders are seen as monsters and saints, pyramid builders and starthrowers. Vivid emphasis is placed on the role of the adult youth leader as a guarantor, an experienced pilgrim walking with younger pilgrims in the pilgrimage of faith. Pilgrim guarantors do not stand still, even though they must take stands—the adult leader can grow as a result of being involved in the ministry with youth (and it is the youth who will stimulate or enable that growth). Pilgrim guarantors take risks, not always knowing the field which adult and youth traverse together. Faithfulness is the compass. As adults give of themselves to youths, risk is very real. Self-giving is always risky.

One of those risks is transference. A young person may transfer his or her problems to the adult, often to the leader who is the most sympathetic listener. This is demon-infested terrain and the adult leader needs the support of the other leaders and a maturity of self-understanding which comes only from a faithful acceptance of the grace of God. Often the adult transfers feelings and fantasies to the young person, again treading on risky terrain. Here it may be the maturity and purity of the young person who offers the saving grace. Many books on youth ministry warn the adult: be true to yourself, do not try to "be a kid." This book says this but also looks personally and deeply to a true self which can incarnate in one's person the love, grace, acceptance, forgiveness, and reconciliation which can be mediated through youth ministry.

Youth ministry is relational. It is an open circle offered to young persons as an alternative to the pyramid they are compelled to climb at school and even at home or church. Young persons are molded by culture to compete, to strive for material and personal success, and to manipulate peers and programs on the way to the top. This is not what Jesus taught. This is not what youth leaders and youth ministry should teach. The alternative vision of a loving, supporting community— a Koinonia—must be modeled. This is a wonderful opportunity for the church to be something that the young people desperately want and did not know existed. Ironically, many adult Christians don't know Koinonia either. In the shift from pyramid to open circle, adults and youth together may discover Koinonia in the form of a gift from God.

To help young people, the adult leaders must be religious. Youth ministry is more than fun and games; through fun and games and many other forms of relationship one pilgrim tells another pilgrim where faith might be found. Adults must be ready to share their faith—often in story form—with the others in the group. Faith stories are told and are heard; adults and youth tell each other. Adults, in the author's view, are also "ritual elders" who help shape sacred space. The leader points out that this is more than a blackberry patch; God is present. The leader helps the group to make rituals—to acknowledge personally and publicly the divine presence. The sentiment of an unintended experience in a blackberry patch is focused and intensified in acts of worship that express the fear, trembling, and gratitude of persons who have been touched by God.

The pattern of this book, dancing to the rhythm of the church year, reminds us that youth ministry is religious and theological. Life revolves around God's creativity and calling. We are God's children and the church is God's colony. While there may be sociological, psychological, and educational aspects to youth ministry, at essence it, like all else in the church, is theological; that is, God- and Christ-centered. This book reminds us of our theological foundations. Youth ministry is incarnational. It is kerygmatic. It is diaconal, and it is revelatory. You may already be practicing these theological principles, perhaps with nontheological names. You are trying to make love real in your own person and in the life of the group. You may be telling the kids that what Jesus was about was restoring our relationship with God and calling us into service to others. All this and more. To know what we are acting upon theological foundations is more than an exercise in naming our actions. It provides our rationale and our impetus. It guards against corruption, and prevents burnout. More adult leaders give up because they don't know why they are doing youth ministry and can't see a destination than for any other reason. This book provides the building materials for a solid theological foundation for youth ministry. The alternative vision of youth ministry as the transformation of persons and communities—the vision of Easter—enables us to build a foundation for the educational, prophetic, pastoral, and liturgical structures which we can design into programs. Of course, the author has in mind tents for pilgrims more than shrines for the established.

What the author has done in this book is what we are asked to do with young people. He has walked with us and pointed out very important signs. He has told us relevant parts of his story, and given us the courage to open up our own stories. By showing respect for us as colleagues in youth ministry, and being creative, Bill Myers has opened up for us new paths as we embark on the pilgrimage of faith, walking with the young persons God has given to us as our companions.

David Ng
Brooklyn, New York
April 1987

Preface

The majority of the chapters contained in this book initially were given as keynote addresses for a "Conference on Theology and Models for Youth Ministry" sponsored by The Alaska Northwest Extension Center of San Francisco Theological Seminary. The leaders of that conference asked me to present themes for youth ministry taken from the liturgical seasons of the church year. When first approached with this unique assignment, I expressed my doubt that the seasons of the church year could provide a useful framework for a youth ministry conference but, as this book suggests, theological themes from the church year are powerful building blocks for a ministry with youth.

I am an ordained Presbyterian Church (USA) minister working in a United Church of Christ Seminary, have a doctorate in Counseling Psychology and have been involved in youth ministry for over twenty-five years. At this point in my life the questions I have about an effective ministry with youth are multifaceted. My concern is engaged when churches claim successful models for youth ministry as places where one adult or, at most, a few adults, are engaged in a ministry *to* instead of *with* youth. Often such a youth program has little or nothing to do with adults in the "big" church; in effect, a parallel "youth church" exists. Often such youth churches seem to imitate cultural agendas. In many of these programs success is determined by the "good" or "bad" statistics of youth fellowships, the deportment of clean-cut fellowship officers, and the winning records of the church's youth basketball leagues. Such practices reflect the competitive forms and the societal norms surrounding the church. I know we can't escape our culture and yet I wonder, with so many cultural promises available to us (compete and you will win; climb and you will be secure; learn and you will earn) what alternative promise can the form, content, and process of a church-based youth *ministry* model intentionally present to youth?

ADVENT's promise (Chapter One) offers an alternative vision for a ministry with youth. The vision is of an inclusive body of people who, as part of the shared process of a community of disciples called together in service, explore and celebrate what the long-awaited coming of the Christchild means for their lives. In this alternative vision, content is the *Advent Promise;* the form is that of a *Christian Community;* and, the process is one of a *Transformative Ministry with* and not *to* youth.

But how does such an alternative vision become reality? In part, the answer to this question has to do with incarnation, the theological theme of CHRISTMAS (Chapter Two). Whenever a church considers the important pieces of a youth ministry model it must start with the incarnational. Key to a church's faithful youth ministry program is the presence of *faithing* adults who incarnate God's love in genuine, appropriate ways. *Faithing* describes the intentional and appropriate activities of those who embody God's love. "To faith" suggests that faith is more of a verb than a noun, more of a total lifestyle than a commodity to be possessed, more of a process than a product. While the presence of such individuals is critical, no less important is what I've come to call *Collective Incarnation;* i.e., the presence of the gathered body of Christ, the congregation, the community of the faithful. All the fancy programs backed by the best resources cannot replace this essential context for youth ministry. Effective youth ministry must be grounded within such an incarnational body of "faithing" persons, a congregation that embodies "good news" by its collective presence.

Within such a congregation, individuals become *Guarantors* for the pilgrimage youth must take. EPIPHANY's (Chapter Three) theological theme concerns that pilgrimage and how adult guarantors become markers in the wilderness guiding those who faithfully journey from youth into adulthood. A guarantor is a kind of living wilderness marker, one who stands as an adult but who also helpfully walks with a youth on his or her journey. Guarantors share the burden of the journey, help read the road maps, raise the hard questions of faith, and offer needed encouragement. They incarnate "adultness" in ways that encourage young people to grow. They embody the faith in a variety of forms. In this way, they "guarantee" the good news that adulthood is feasible and that the Christian story is also their story. Guarantors who intentionally stand within the Christian tradition know Christ as the perfect guarantor; i.e., Christ's story is the adult story within which "I" make sense out of "my" pilgrimage and how "I" am to journey with youth.

But adults, even Christian guarantors, have what I've come to call the *shadowside*. The shadowside has to do with the broken places, the unresolved adolescent places, the still present (though often deeply buried) bruises and hurts which sometimes overwhelm adult guarantors. Jesus had his moments of temptation, and in the LENTEN (Chapter Four) theme some of the shadowside temptations of youth ministry are addressed. There is, unfortunately, much to talk about here; nevertheless, Chapters Three through Five affirm that adults within a lively "faithing" church can incarnate good news for youth from their stance as individual and collective guarantors even as they wrestle with their own (and the church's) shadowsides.

As Lent resolves itself on EASTER (Chapter Five), the theological theme of *Transformation* occurs, and those who experience the Christ's transformative Easter claim in their lives are never the same again. Unfortunately, youth ministry has too often failed in locating, consecrating, and stewarding such transformative space. We've been good at designing programs for youth ministry which require blocks of time devoted to a thematic exploration of worship, but such efforts, as well as the church's annual Youth Sunday productions, have been, for the most part, ceremonial celebrations of the status quo. And, while we have recruited adults to work with youth, rarely have we been about the business of being ritual elders, adults who not only incarnate good news as guarantors, but who also accept the ritual responsibility to intentionally locate, while on pilgrimage with youth, those places from the journey which can become sacred containers consecrated and held in trust for *Easter Moments* in which transformative space occurs. Such space cannot be controlled or commanded; it can only be invoked.

For those involved in youth ministry, the companion

process to such an invocation of sacred space is the actual doing of *Practical Theology* (Chapter Six: the theological theme of PENTECOST). "Doing practical theology" happens when a community of faith focuses upon the variety of issues discovered in the midst of pilgrimage. Such issues are held up to the community and then considered through the dual lens of the culture and the Christian tradition. An intentional design occurs out of the warrants chosen from both Christianity and culture, resulting in an action which is critiqued and, if appropriate, continued.

Actions are structured attempts by the community to reach toward systemic and personal transformations. As such, whatever actions occur are claimed as *confessional moments* through which theological and cultural understandings hopefully are shared with ever larger communities. Such actions might occur *educationally:* for example, as a senior high peer staff designs an action for a junior high confirmation class; or might occur *prophetically:* for example, in the confrontative action by older youth around the hiring practices of a church; or might occur *pastorally:* for example, by high school and college-age youth setting up and staffing a hot-line suicide-prevention center; or, might occur *liturgically:* for example, by youth and adults leading a Sunday worship celebration; but, whatever action occurs, the implication of the model is transformation. Such transformative action, guided by both theological and cultural reflection, moves not only youth but the entire community of faith forward on its pilgrimage.

Chapter Seven *(ALL HALLOWS EVE and ALL SAINTS' DAY)* sketches a somewhat different picture of youth ministry from today's "mainline" denominational churches. In contrast to what has been presented above as an effective model for a congregation's ministry *with* youth, most contemporary settings seem to imply that:

1) *worship* is something done only by adults; 2) *community* means "our" youth group; 3) *Christian education* means the transfer of information, most of it irrelevant; 4) *ministry* is something done only by adult professionals; 5) *conversion,* or any radical claim by Christ, is silly nonsense; and, 6) *nurture* is to be understood as social "fun time" centered in youth fellowship programs. While we are the inheritors of this historical chain of events, we need not accept it uncritically. Reminding us that All Saints' Day is the day on which most congregations traditionally honor their "saints" who have died in the past year ("saints" is used in the biblical sense to include all faithful believers), Chapter Seven goes on to note that such an understanding of "saint" surely includes those adolescents who believe; i.e., youth are important members of congregations.

Contemporary congregations need to open their doors to the vitality of ministry *with* youth. Effective ministry *with* youth is based inside congregations that incarnate the Christian gospel in lively ways. In such congregations adult guarantors can work *with* youth in an ongoing process that moves through an ever-expanding cultural dialogue into transformative action. In addition, ritual elders from the congregation locate, within this ongoing pilgrimage, the sacred spaces for transformative worship. The congregation acts out its theology of ministry *with* youth in everything from how church windows are cleaned to how Communion is served. Here is where the Advent promise is incarnated among the saints; here, too, is where that same promise is broken, buried, and resurrected.

My hope is that this book prompts a reconsideration of the role of the congregation in transformative ministry *with* youth. I also hope the pragmatic agenda of this book is understood. The forms we choose to build upon as we design our youth ministry programs make a difference and "provoking sacred space" is a frightening task not lightly undertaken. The confessional acts we, as a congregation, choose to live by, anchor our pilgrimage in weak or profound ways. In all of this, we will continue our pilgrimage, knowing the Advent promise will be kept.

1

The Promise: ADVENT

When we wait for a promise to be fulfilled . . . wait for, once more, God's presence with us, enfleshed. The mood of Advent is one of watchful expectancy. Now the gray, dark chill of winter imperceptibly retreats before the slowly lengthening light—light that encourages the possibility of spring. In the midst of darkness the Advent cry is heard—"Come, Lord Jesus, Come!"—and we witness a miracle: God keeps the promise.

And yet, as always, there is a problem. The problem has to do with another source of light. The theologian Gabriel Fackre puts it for us in today's terminology: "The overcast skies of the late twentieth century color all the future we see in Advent perspective. The doomsday clock of nuclear proliferation is four minutes to midnight. From the light that comes from that day there will be no hiding place."[1] Advent, a time of waiting. Waiting for, shall we say, either God's presence with us enfleshed as the Prince of Peace or the destruction of all flesh by mushroom-shaped clouds.

In the face of such a hopeless vision, the Advent lectionary points toward Isaiah. The prophet speaks of no more war, of people beating "their swords into plowshares and their spears into pruning hooks" (Isaiah 2:4). And Isaiah takes us up the mountain where we see nations flowing to the house of the Lord. On that mountain a judgment is rendered: "Neither shall they learn war any more." This is Isaiah's vision, and because we understand this vision to be true, action is demanded. For Christians to speak of Advent in our time is to embody the hope-filled vision of the Prince of Peace.

This vision is the "nevertheless" of the Bible. Do we speak of MX missiles or war budgets? *Nevertheless*, our waiting at Advent is a waiting for a promise, God's presence with us, enfleshed as a vision of peace. We may fail, but the Advent promise of Christ's coming never fails, and is the backdrop of our every effort. We have this gift, we are called to share it. *Nevertheless*. And what does this have to do with youth ministry?

In a large way, these alternative visions—on the one hand, the bomb; on the other, lasting peace—state the parameters of ministry in our age. In a much narrower way these alternative visions call into question the goals and the forms youth ministry takes.

What is youth ministry about? Is it about a journey toward the ultimate "no" underlying the mushroom cloud or is it about a pilgrimage into the "yes" of the Advent promise underlying all of life?

I read a lot. I especially respect Ray Bradbury. His novels and short stories examine life and do so with power. Let me share with you Bradbury's beautiful passage from his book *Dandelion Wine* in which two twelve-year-old boys are outside wrestling when one of them, Douglas, is knocked out. We tune in as Douglas comes to and discovers himself, really discovers himself, for the first time. He says, in awe, "I'm alive!" And then:

> The grass whispered under his body. He put his arm down, feeling the sheath of fuzz on it, and, far away, below, his toes creaking in his shoes. The wind sighed over his shelled ears. The world slipped bright over the glassy round of his eyeballs like images sparked in a crystal sphere. Flowers were sun and fiery spots of sky strewn through the woodland. Birds flickered like skipped stones across the vast inverted pond of heaven. His breath raked over his teeth, going in ice, coming out fire. Insects shocked the air with electric clearness. Ten thousand individual hairs grew a millionth of an inch on his head. He heard the twin hearts beating in each ear, the third heart beating in his throat, the two hearts throbbing his wrists, the real heart pounding his chest. The million pores on his body opened.
>
> I'm *really* alive! he thought. I never knew it before, or if I did I don't remember!
>
> He yelled it loud but silent, a dozen times! Think of if, think of it! Twelve years old and only now! Now discovering this rare timepiece, this clock gold-bright and guaranteed to run threescore and ten, left under a tree and found while wrestling. . . .
>
> [The two boys] spilled downhill, the sun in their mouths, in their eyes like shattered lemon glass, gasping like trout thrown out on a bank, laughing till they cried. . . .
>
> [Then Douglas's friend Tom asked:] "Doug, you're not mad?" . . . [And Douglas, responding, said] "No, no, no, no, no!"
>
> Douglas, eyes shut, saw spotted leopards pad in the dark.

3

"Tom!" Then quieter, "Tom . . . does everyone in the world . . . knows he's alive?"

"Sure. Heck, yes!"

The leopards trotted soundlessly off through darker lands where eyeballs could not turn to follow.

"I hope they do," whispered Douglas. "Oh, I sure hope they know."[2]

Doug responds to what I call the promise of Advent, the "yes," the "nevertheless" underlying all of life. He has had a moment in which this striking *yes* has been affirmed, personally, for him. And he knows it! Yes, he says, life is worth living. In spite of all the evil I am really alive and this world is a miracle of affirmation, of goodness . . . and I sure hope everyone in the world knows.

For those of us who know *whose* we are, such moments suggest, when we talk about ministry with youth, that youth ministry is *not* something for the kids to keep them busy. It's *not* something to protect or innoculate youth against the rigors of the world. It's *not* the way we capture members for the church, either for now or for the future, as in "work with youth because they are our future." No; youth ministry is pilgrimage with those youth who are journeying—some faithfully, others with immense fear—but everyone, including ourselves, on a pilgrimage in *this* world. Ray Bradbury's young friend Douglas, tumbling down a grassy bank, aware—finally aware—of the yes underlying all of life. Well, I want, as a youth minister, to be on a pilgrimage with youth in such ways that moments like Doug's are affirmed. I believe I am called, as a Christian youth minister, to such a pilgrimage with youth interacting with the yes underlying all of life. But how? My hunch is that our tradition offers us markers for such a journey, if we can see them. Consider, for example, the *koinonia circle.*

4

THE OPEN CIRCLE OF KOINONIA
OR THE DOMINANT CULTURE'S PYRAMID

Koinonia is the New Testament Greek word for ministry as togetherness, fellowship, participation, communion, or community. We've come to think of Koinonia as the small group within the church, but Koinonia is a word for people who are in the process of coming together as co-ministers, as "priests to each other."[3] Through the Koinonia process, those who know *whose* they are become Christ's body and embody the Advent promise. The form this embodiment takes is that of the open circle. Anyone—in fact, everyone—is called to the faith community of the open circle. Here faith is noted by how we love one another. This marker, the marker of the Koinonia community, is not really honored in our culture. Instead, we honor other markers. For example, Tom Wolfe's book *The Right Stuff* speaks of the intense climb of America's astronauts to be "the right stuff." Wolfe describes their arena—that of the top test pilot— as a game in which the opponent is death:

> ". . . The idea here (in the all-enclosing fraternity) seemed to be that a man should have the ability to go up in a hurtling piece of machinery and put his hide on the line and then have the moxie, the reflexes, the experience, the coolness, to pull it back in the last yawning moment—and then to go up again *the next day,* and the next day, and every next day, even if the series should prove infinite—and, ultimately, in its best expression, do so in a cause that means something to thousands, to a people, a nation, to humanity, to God. Nor was there *a test* to show whether or not a pilot had this righteous quality. There was, instead, a seemingly infinite series of tests. A career in flying was like climbing one of those ancient Babylonian pyramids made up of a dizzy progression of steps

5

and ledges, a ziggurat, a pyramid extraordinarily high and steep; and the idea was to prove at every foot of the way up that pyramid that you were one of the elected and anointed ones who had *the right stuff* and could move higher and higher and even—ultimately, God willing, one day—that you might be able to join that special few at the very top, that elite who had the capacity to bring tears to men's eyes, the very Brotherhood of the Right Stuff itself."[4]

Most high schools enculturate in this way. Youth understand. Instead of an open Koinonia circle there is the *right stuff* pyramid. This form—in grades, sports, athletics, drama, choir, band—overlaps and interlocks in subtle ways. Designed with competition in mind, the high school is tied to its culture. Competition is a cultural value undergirded by complementary values like position, material acquisition, and power. These values are what finally determine the high school's educational form—a series of *right stuff* interlocking pyramids which allow only a select few to reach the top. The end goal of education is articulated as *success*. Survive the competition and you will succeed. You will receive the "A," the "best athlete," or "most popular" award. School is to be understood by youth as a mirror of real life: beat the other person or get beaten yourself. Survive. Compete. The unwritten expectation is to get to the top of at least one pyramid.

The encouragement of this form—competitive interlocking *right stuff* pyramids—is the fault of no one and the fault of everyone. The reality of the high school is that competitive pyramids exist, and that regardless of where one person is within the pyramids, playing this game is seen as an acceptable way of life. Here, worth is determined by success; that is, by how one continually keeps on top.

I believe that the collective pyramids are more than

school. They are the end result of the home, the church, the culture—the end result of the American dream of having the right stuff and *making it*. The school brings the pyramid form sharply into focus because it is here that the job of teaching what life is all about in our society is to take place. And that job is being done. "Everyone accepts the pyramid as the only game worth playing; there seems to be no acceptable alternative. So it is that [countless youth move daily] between classes, each one a cog within a thousand competitive pyramids. The halls are alive with milling bodies, each one crying for affirmation, love, just a touch . . . please . . . and the doors close."[5]

Most youth ministers have not recognized the importance of either this marker or its form. What we have usually done is to duplicate the competitive pyramid in church school and youth group clothing. The church school has classes and the youth group has officers; a selected few assist the minister; we note with pride those who succeed in the school pyramids; certain church offices become stepping stones toward the highest positions in the church's session or governing board; i.e., the top of the church pyramid. When this happens, the values of the pyramid are reinforced. The hoped-for communication of love, wholeness, individuality, and competence infrequently occurs. What is learned is that the pyramid is real and that the words offered by the church are phony. Love, and all that stuff, can then be viewed as sloppy sentimentalism.

I want to state, in opposition to the stance of the pyramid, that we are on a pilgrimage with youth and that our tradition can help faithfully inform that journey. If we journey faithfully we will struggle to be *less* of a "Right Stuff" pyramid where success is measured by competition and *more* of a "Koinonia open circle" where success is measured by how we minister, love and care for ourselves and others. How are we to do this?

7

PERSONAL KERYGMAS OR THE CHRISTIAN KERYGMA

Kerygma, the word proclaimed, is ministry articulated and is the proclamation of the good news in all its forms. Kerygma is more than preaching. Inherent within it is the teaching (Didache) ministry of the people of God; it rotates out of profound religious language in word, metaphor, story, and symbol. "Jesus is Lord," an early Kerygmatic statement, can be embodied in many ways, but if this is to be youth ministry, then an authentic Christian Kerygmatic stance—an embodied proclamation—should be visible.

Let me be confessional at this point and share what I might call two *personal Kerygmas:* Growing up in the tumbledown hills and deer-filled woods of northwestern Pennsylvania meant learning the words and the skills for camping and killing. So I learned how to shoot a gun and pitch a tent, how to skin a deer and how to build a canoe. As hunters we sat around campfires and spoke of the deer who, gutshot, ran five miles, wheezing crimson onto the white snow. And we posed in front of our tents, victoriously carried our kills home and ate canned venison. On occasions we would, in flights of fancy, consider ourselves to be very much like the old-time hunters. Clearly this personal Kerygma suggested that I would be saved by "doing what a man's gotta do" out there in the woods of Pennsylvania.

I'm also trained in Counseling Psychology. I know about empathy and the fifty-minute hour. I have no fear of one-on-one encounters and the dynamics of groups in process fascinate me. I understand the jargon of this profession and I carefully maintain my professional connections. This second personal Kerygma suggested that I would be saved by being "self-actualized" and "congruent with my positive inner core."

Inside myself I may have merged both of these Kerygmas. Indeed, they have, for me, great salvific power. One Kerygmatic vision seems to come straight from the movie *The Deer Hunter* and calls for "doing what a man's gotta do." The second Kerygmatic vision comes straight from Carl Rogers and Abraham Maslow[6]: I am "self-actualized" and I have a "therapeutic personality." I am laid back and a warm fuzzy. When I merge these two visions I have a possible marker which could become, for me, a personal kerygmatic proclamation and a framework for how I carry out youth ministry.

Let's consider: If this marker holds power, what would it look like? In the "First Church of the Warm Fuzzy Deer Hunter" (that's a pretty good name) we might have several small discussion/encounter/ self-help groups meeting regularly and a fellowship group marked by much volleyball and fun. The fall retreat will deal with "caring for each other" and the spring retreat will deal with "holding on and letting go." Summertime will be set aside for a major canoe trip and/or hike with a special camp-out weekend for Junior Highs.

The kind of language the laid back warm fuzzy *person* (emphasize person) uses in this marker, this Kerygmatic vision, is a mixture of psychology and camping terminology. Youth come away from my program able to reflectively listen and to identify how many feet are in a canoe trip's portage rod and to emphathetically understand while reading a compass during a driving rainstorm.

This personal vision also develops a shared story that includes the time Jason made pancakes on a retreat in an old house and the fuse popped; the time the bears entered camp and ate the butter; and the time, on the canoe trip, John almost got hit with lightning.

This personal Kerygmatic vision of the Church of the Warm Fuzzy Deer Hunter also provides *symbols* for our journey: a canoe paddle gets mounted in the youth room with all the canoe trip dates burned into its wood;

pictures from the retreat are thumbtacked to that same wall; and one big poster shows a youth and an adult (maybe his dad) playing volleyball. And there are several awards from the church's young men's basketball league sitting in the very visible trophy case.

Now don't get me wrong! In this Church of the Warm Fuzzy Deer Hunter there have been *ritual sharings* and moments of mystery (like the time we all sat on a rock watching the Northern Lights over Long Knife Lake in Southern Canada). But is this ministry? Some may well argue it is. But where are the Christian Kergymatic statements, the embodiment of the Advent gift? I do *not* sense that my personal cultural Kerygmas, my vision of the warm fuzzy deer hunter and his merry band of men playing volleyball and canoeing in Southern Canada is any better than the cultural pyramid or can legitimately replace the Christian Kerygma. Our faith makes this audacious claim: It is the Christian Kerygma that comprises the pillars of smoke and fire, the warrants, *the* actual vision of what all ministry should entail. Kerygma is the claim that Jesus is Lord, and youth ministry has to do with how the Advent promise which grounds us comes into the world of every youth.

Every Sunday we confess that we have seen *the vision* and failed to live as God in Christ has called us to live. In a sense, every week we promise once again to start over—to begin again—to live within the vision. We pledge that we ourselves will go forth and gift the world with love. This would be a joke, an absurdity, except that we are the receivers, the recipients of a gift that will not go away. Christ gifts us with himself again and again and again. And he goes with us as we, in our stumbling uncertain ways, attempt to gift others with this promise of abundant life. We may fail, but the actual vision, the Advent promised Christ event, never fails and is the backdrop of our every effort. We have this gift; we are called to share it.

I'm suggesting that youth ministry, to be theologically consistent with the Christian tradition, should be more like an open circle and less like a culture's competitive pyramid; it should be more involved with the Christian Kerygmatic proclamation and less involved with personal Kerygmatic proclamations. But there is a third marker for the journey.

DIAKONIA MINISTRY *WITH* AND NOT *TO* YOUTH

Diakonia, the Greek word meaning service, is the root of a variety of words in the New Testament used in reference to the Apostles, to every believer, and to special forms of ministry. The New Testament notes different functions of ministry—teachers, bishops, deacons, presbyters, and evangelists—but expects diakonia, *service,* from everyone. Moltmann, in emphasizing Jesus as the one unique high priest, suggests "the community of the baptized is the community of those who have been called. There are no differences here. All are called and commissioned."[7] *All* are to serve. Here, again, Advent vision becomes flesh. Here, again, Advent vision becomes embodied community action. There is a holistic vision here: the community has within itself the resources necessary to serve; it is the entire people of God, the community of faith, which serves. When chaos breaks in, the *community* responds. Not one person, but rather the community! ALL serve. There may well be different forms of service, but *all* serve.

I have long suggested that ministry *with* youth should be an operating metaphor for youth ministry. Here the community asks member youth to serve. Not by themselves, but as part of the community. So a high school junior and a senior might help a lay person and the

11

pastor teach and lead a confirmation group. Such service, such ministry, makes excellent sense, given our understanding of Diakonia. Some of this service is occasional, some is regularized, but there are many hints as to the presence of this Diakonia service. Do youth serve on official boards? Do they pledge? Are they occasional lay readers on Sunday? If there is a youth committee, are half of its members youth? Do older youth care for younger youth in this community? Does the church community reach, via its youth, outside the church? Are there intergenerational teaching staffs? Whatever the form, such all-hands-involved service embodies Diakonia ministry. In this community all are called to serve, including youth. Mitch, a high school senior, had this to say in church the day he graduated: "Soon I'll be leaving this place, but not really. You will go with me. You treated me like a real person. I argued with you, prayed with you, and even preached with you. You helped me when I was hurting, and I believe I helped you when I could see your hurt. I was a teacher for the confirmation program and a regular participant in worship. Those were the sharing places that helped me grow. Thank you for helping me grow." A compelling vision.

But in the field education department of the seminary where I work, 85 percent of new concurrent parish field placements desire young seminarians to serve as "hired guns" in either Christian education or in ministry *to* youth positions. These churches have a solution for youth ministry. I call it the Lone Ranger Syndrome. Too often the church seems to want the seminarian to be the *professional* hired to solve what is a big problem: what do we do with youth? This is *Lone Ranger* leadership. In this metaphor there is a distressful, chaotic situation existing with which people cannot cope; they need help. The Lone Ranger and trusted assistant Tonto enter, assess the situation and act, decisively and effectively, expending silver bullets from their well-stocked gun belts. With order restored, both depart, leaving behind a rejoicing people. Hi Ho Silver, away!

Such a scenario, for the short run, is effective. It is in the long run that such leadership becomes a toxic metaphor for community and for Diakonia service. With only one leader in charge, the community remains convicted of their inability to function without the leader's continual presence. Others, dreaming of glory instead of considering service, dare to adopt the dream, becoming proficient Lone Ranger clones carrying saddlebags crammed with silver bullets. Such leadership encourages a format of ministry *to* instead of co-ministry *with* youth.

Consider the power of foot-washing. Foot-washing exemplifies ministry as Diakonia service inside and outside the open Koinonia community circle. In such a process, people, young and old alike, can co-minister, becoming priests for each other. In this way laity remain the "Laos," the people of God, while embodying the incarnational presence of Christ. And, when every person is a priest, *everyone has been graced with silver bullets.* Leadership skill no longer resides with just the professional minister. All can serve, and can serve well.

That we hold onto the Lone Ranger model is an indictment of seminary training and church expectation. That professional youth ministers remain in positions an average of two to three years suggests the worth of the model. We need to critically explore the inherent possibilities of shared ministry. We need to consider youth as potential co-ministers and not as objects to be manipulated. And such service (Dakonia) finally points beyond the church, not within it.

When I consider these markers for our pilgrimage, the marker of *Koinonia community,* the marker of *Kerygmatic Proclamation* and the marker of *Diakonia Service,* I am reminded of Ross Snyder's five questions, with which he summed up youth ministry:

13

1. Is it possible to put together a life world instead of a death world?
2. Is there a power that can overcome and transform the chaos and confusion which keep coming at me?
3. Will I ever realize my promise? What is it?
4. What words, images, stories, could enable me to make sense out of me and what is happening?
5. Is there somewhere a warm body of people who believe in each other—and in something together? In which I could be a first-class citizen?[8]

And I want to shout "Yes" to all five questions. Yes, it is possible to put together a life world instead of a death world. And yes, there is a power, a source, a personal presence that overcomes and can help me transform the chaos which keeps coming at me. And yes, youth can realize their promise and can find it. And yes, there are words, images, and stories which can feed us as we journey. And yes, there is here, on this journey, a warm body of people who are coming to believe in each other and in something together. They—together—are baking warm bread for their pilgrimage. Come, for we have far to go, and you are needed.

2

Incarnation:
CHRISTMAS

At Christmas we remember the *actual vision*, the incarnation, the assumption of human form by God in Jesus Christ. Thinking of the incarnation, W. H. Auden penned these lines for Christmas:

> Once again
> As in previous years we have seen the actual
>   Vision and failed
> To do more than entertain it as an agreeable
> Possibility, once again we have sent Him away,
> Begging though to remain His disobedient
>   servant,
> The promising child who cannot keep His word
>   for long.[1]

15

Auden's line says we are, at Christmas, "the promising child who cannot keep His word for long." We are like small promising children at Christmas entertaining—just for a moment—the actual possibility of what Christ could mean in our lives. But then we send him away, unable to invite him into the rest of our existence. Christmas is only an agreeable possibility. There could be peace. There could be justice. There could be food on every table this day and every day. There could be, but "as in previous years we have seen the actual Vision and failed . . . once again we have sent him away."

INCARNATION OF THE "ROUGH BEAST"

Another visionary, William Butler Yeats, wrote about what we might put in place of the *actual vision*. In his poem "The Second Coming," Yeats describes a "rough beast," shaped "with lion body and the head of a man," slouching toward Bethlehem to be finally born after "twenty centuries of stony sleep." Listen to his words:

> . . .somewhere in the sands of the desert
> A shape with lion body and the head of a man,
> A gaze blank and pitiless as the sun,
> Is moving its slow thighs, while all about it
> Reel shadows of the indignant desert birds.
> The darkness drops again; but now I know
> that twenty centuries of stony sleep
> Were vexed to nightmare by a rocking cradle,
> And what rough beast, its hour come round at
> last,
> Slouches towards Bethlehem to be born?[2]

Many such "rough beasts" are incarnated in moments of hopelessness, in images of despair, in options of defeat and alienation. And what do these two images—the *actual vision* and the *rough beast*—say about ministry with youth? I think of the guy who does drugs before arriving at a youth program. I know he smokes grass. He knows I know it. I know he knows I know. What now? Forget it? Hardly. Because I *know* his situation, his family, the people he hangs with, and his pain. I *know* him and this is a critical moment in my ministry with him; am I afraid, or will I name his pain and play it out, all the while empathizing with that pain? Or, I see tears in the eyes of a girl and I know her in her suffering. I hurt to watch her (and again, this is a critical point in my ministry with her). Will I avoid her, or will I say to her, "I know you and you are in pain and I'd like to listen to what's going on in your world." What will I do?

The powers of darkness and the principalities of despair are real. Of that I have no doubt whatsoever. Many "rough beasts" are being born. Today the principalities of despair have more acceptable labels, as do the powers of darkness, but they exist. We might sanitize them, for example, by calling them "systems": economic systems, political systems, even family systems can be evil. I speak of the "rough beasts" of family abuse, of economic deprivation, of things like drugs, gangs, and teen-age pregnancies as the logical consequences of such systems. Such rough beasts slouch toward Bethlehem. Pain and despair are real. Evil has power. Such rough beasts are being born all around us if we but have eyes to see.

OUR STARTING POINT: INCARNATING THE "GOOD NEWS"

And yet, when Christ says "Come and see" in the gospel of John (1:39) he invites us to see the presence of the kingdom all around us. This—the presence of the kingdom—is the good news! The Jews had hoped that this might be true, that God's kingdom might come some day. But Christ announced that it had happened, that God's kingdom was here, now! To see with the eyes of faith means to see that things have been altered, that evil is not in charge, that deep within reality lies a "yes" instead of a "no."

If youth ministry is to seriously consider the incarnational claim of Christmas, the *actual vision*, then my first question to someone considering an active ministry with youth might well be: Are you genuine in your faith claims? Or, is leadership a mask you put on to keep people out of your life? Are you what you appear to be? Or, is what you appear to be totally different from what you are? For example: is the truth of Genesis your truth? Have you lived Noah's flooded moment when all was watery chaos and there was no firm earth on which to stand; and, miracle of miracles, a dove came with a green branch and settled lightly in your hand so that you knew hope, rainbow hope? Are such faith-filled stories *your* story? Am "I" genuine in my faith claim, or am "I" hiding behind my mask from the risk of life? *Genuine.* I am what I appear to be. I am in constant touch with the "Yes" that has impacted me, formed my identity, created my faith.

Whenever we consider the important pieces of a youth ministry model we must start with the incarnational. The key to good youth ministry, faithful youth ministry, is the presence of genuine faithing adults who incarnate God's love in appropriate ways. I once sat with a group of youth who were interviewing seminarians, hoping to select one who would be a Field Education student in their church for the year. In the midst of the interview, one rigid seminarian spoke of his theology of trusting in God's love and loving his neighbor as he loved himself. The words were perfect, but when several youth questioned this young man on his "story," the truth of the matter appeared to be that at no point in his adult life had this seminarian been caringly involved with youth—or perhaps anyone—on any profound level. He seemed to be at the interview because a well-intentioned faculty member felt he needed some practical experience. Academically he had nearly straight "As" but all the words, while correct, didn't connect. Somehow he wasn't real and yet he wanted to minister to youth. Ten minutes into the interview a seventh-grade girl across the room caught my eye and motioned thumbs down. She knew; I knew; the faculty member who suggested this experience to the seminarian knew; and, I have to believe the seminarian knew, too. Incarnation. Incarnation of what—the good news, or some feared and fearful rough beast slouching toward Bethlehem? Note well: the key to youth ministry is the presence of genuine adults who are faithful in appropriate ways, who are not hiding from life.

INCARNATION AND THE INDIVIDUAL

Because I speak of youth ministry as persons faithfully present, I tell stories. I remember three ministers from when I grew up; not one had large youth problems, but they were important people for me. One had a hobby of deep involvement in the local Boy Scout program. Often he'd go canoeing with me and my friends. Each morning we would lock canoes together for a brief prayer and his presentation of a "word for the day." He would ask us to think about the word and then, much later, we'd sit around the campfire reflecting on our word. The words? I remember *fire, land, work, food,* and *water.* These words helped us frame our experience so that we could see the presence of the "yes" that is the kingdom round about us. Certainly this person incarnated good news for me. I felt the presence, if you will, of Auden's *actual vision.*

My second minister was a biker who matched biblical imagery with what it is like to bike long distances on hot days. Such biking was truly a wilderness experience. He helped us see manna and water in the wilderness . . . burning bushes before our eyes . . . tired feet and a foot-washing celebration . . . Communion . . . grains of wheat, crushed, fired, exploded, and miracle of miracles—bread! Yes, we could *see* the kingdom. In fact, after sixty miles up and down hills many of us discovered God's presence in water spilled from a friendly farmer's garden hose. Again, here was a person who incarnated good news for me. Again, a sense of Auden's *actual vision*.

My third minister was a man who wore red socks under his robe, along with his clerical collar complete with formal white Geneva Tabs. He couldn't ride a bike and certainly never entered a canoe, but he could listen. And his whole youth ministry was just that: to intentionally sit and listen. Twice each year he would individually sit with every youth from his congregation, usually over a coke in a local ice cream shop. And the day my younger brother tossed two firecrackers into the school auditorium, this red-socked minister was called in by my angry mother. Sitting with my brother, this man told my brother how he had, in college, gotten into similar trouble. For me, that empathic connection remains an incarnational example of what ministry with youth entails—caring concern on the part of adults who not only listen, but who care, and care appropriately. He, too, in his own way, helped me *see* the kingdom. He also incarnated good news.

One more story: a congregation hired a seminarian who was a woodworker. Opening this side of his life to and with youth, he used images from the Bible to work into wood. In this conversational way he carved symbols of faith and offered them in their unfinished state so that youth might discuss them and help him complete them. And a strange thing happened: people related to his way of being, recognized his realness and his sharing of himself so that one day a group of boys offered to the community a sun-bleached log for a Communion table and another young man drilled holes into that table inside which notes of care from people were carefully placed and sealed with wooden plugs during a worship celebration. And when the woodworker left this congregation he carried a homemade banner, an antique carpenter's rule, and a book of poetry about God's image of "yes" in our world—all gifts given to him by youth in response to his genuineness. He, too, incarnated Christmas good news. He, too, enabled me to glimpse Auden's *actual vision*.

COLLECTIVE INCARNATION AND THE CONGREGATION

Good youth ministry models are collective incarnational places where a number of adults incarnate God's presence in appropriately authentic ways, each person living faithfully in response to the "yes" of life. All the fancy programs, the resources, the buildings, and the ski trips cannot replace this essential starting point—the presence of faithful adults who incarnate good news by their very presence. But how can we get faithing adults and youth *incarnationally together* as the "Laos," the "people of God," the "actual vision," the *whole* "body of Christ"? Let's consider a story about *Collective Incarnation*.

A pastor once was called to a church congregation which had eight youth. Eight youth. And youth ministry was to have some priority. That initial year started with a setting aside of two hours each month for intentional one-on-one listening meetings with individual youth. In four months eight youth had been individually listened to by the pastor. When eight months had passed, this pastor had spent two quality listening hours with every youth in the congregation! By the end of the first year the pastor had spent three hours with each youth, listening!

The second step for this pastor's beginning of a new youth program was to have lunch with the school superintendent. When the pastor asked for permission to occasionally eat lunch in the school cafeteria with several youth from the congregation, the superintendent said O.K. and, in addition, once a month the pastor managed to visit art class before and history class after the lunch period. In this way the pastor was able to spend roughly the equivalent of one full day in the local high school over the course of an entire school year.

The pastor then evaluated what the church called a confirmation class. That first year the pastor had inherited a Saturday morning class of three seventh graders. Everyone who had taken that confirmation class in seventh grade now, as older youth, moaned about its uselessness. In this second year the pastor maintained the seventh grade confirmation class, ran a few additional youth events and continued to meet with individual youth. During the next summer the pastor asked the one senior and the one junior in the church to join with the pastor and two adult advisors in a new confirmation program. These five persons—two adult advisors, the pastor, the senior, and the junior—were to regularly plan for and then meet with the six youth found in grades six to ten over a Sunday breakfast in the church. The staff of five would plan the program once a month over pizza in one of the advisor's homes. In that setting, all program ideas, retreat possibilities, and major projects would be discussed, but the central focus would always be this question: "How does the Christian faith impact on us now, today? And how can we share this with our breakfast group?"

Much later the pastor told me that this Sunday breakfast group led those youth to a deep involvement with

Sunday congregational worship. Initially they were at the fringes of such worship, ushering and occasionally reading scripture, but slowly the breakfast group started to utilize worship as the focal point of their program. Sermons were discussed before and after they were given. On two occasions blocks of time were spent by the group to plan the totality of Sunday worship, including a ninth grader's presentation of the sermon. Several times other adults were invited to breakfast to share their stories. One of those meetings led to the youth providing leg power for a critical vote on a family shelter issue in their hometown. Over the summer this group also provided staff for the neighborhood vacation church school and, with the help of a doctor in the congregation, staffed a much needed medical clinic on wheels. Because of pastoral and adult support of this program by the congregation this breakfast group began to always be involved with worship.

The pastor tells me that once a year the group takes a "rites of passage" retreat. After being some place for two nights while writing statements of faith, Sunday morning finds this rites-of-passage group back in the Sunday worship service, centering on the one or two seniors who will soon be leaving. While parents and members of the group are called forward to stand round the seniors and lay hands on them as a blessing, the pastor invokes God's continued presence with them on their pilgrimage. There is, says the pastor, "much singing and celebrating on these beautiful Sundays."

John Westerhoff talks about the faithful people of God, the congregation, that little company of pilgrims, as the place where *enculturation* occurs—not indoctrination, but enculturation.[3] Here, deep within the faithing congregation, is where the birthing of hope happens. An incarnational model for ministry with youth centers in just such a faithing congregation. If we take incarnation seriously, then the hidden curriculum of our model includes the potlucks, the Christmas pageants, the people, the place itself, and the prayers and songs and actions of the congregation. The congregation that is being faithful is the best model for youth ministry. Such a congregation will celebrate the kingdom of God's presence in unique ways, and there will be laughter and circles of touching, caring adults. In this time and place, individual incarnational ministry with youth is grounded in that collective incarnational "body of Christ" we call the congregation.

BEING PRESENT INCARNATIONALLY

Being fully present incarnationally means being present physically. There is something about the incarnation—something about God made flesh, present with us—that takes shape in the bear hug of a college male after an eight-hundred-mile bike hike when he says, "We made it!" And his embrace feels good. There is also truth in the gentle kiss given by an eighty-two-year-old woman following a sermon that touched her. And there is appropriate caring and warmth as the incarnational body of Christ celebrates with youth and adults standing in a circle, arms on shoulders, singing Shalom or, in that same circle, when persons stand crying as hands are placed upon the shoulders and arms of some who are struggling with anger, pain, and loss. In such ways *we* collectively incarnate our celebration of the "yes" of life, even in the midst of tragedy. Then "we," as faithful congregation, are fully present.

The church groups where I feel most at home are groups where incarnational human touch is a critical ingredient. The *touch* I speak of here is a touching not forced or demanded or laden with inappropriate messages, but a spontaneous and genuine, for the most part, expression of love. I say "for the most part," because every group has moments when people pose, wear masks, or do what they think the group expects them to do. Here "rough beasts" raise their heads. I also say "for the most part" because occasional fantasies do cross the minds of adults working with youth and are then, if one has a covenant for the long haul, put aside; but without *touch* one loses the full sense of incarnational ministry. What am I to do, without touch, when a young man has lost his father? Only incarnationally can I share the tears. What am I to do, without touch, when a young woman enters my space dancing with joy? Only incarnationally can I share the laughter. What are we, as a group—the body of Christ—to do, without touch, when we pray our concerns and our joys for specific members? Only incarnationally can we share the actual vision that heals, that provides hope.

Stephen D. Jones in *Faith Shaping*, argues that we incarnate faith to youth by *nearness* and *directness*. By *nearness* Jones means that the church as a faith community must provide a closeness to that community and its traditions, rituals, and stories. Jones says:

> The faith is near when Christian adults live their faith in natural ways before the young person. The faith is near when the young person feels that he or she is a close part of the church. The faith is near when the young person is allowed deep relationships with adult Christian models. The faith is near when families are not embarrassed to express faith and when parents are public with their commitments. The faith is near when families develop and practice faithful traditions in the home with regularity. The faith is near when youth can see how much faith is prized by the important adults around them.[4]

Nearness is another way of using Bushnell's idea of *nurture*, so that children grow never knowing that they are anything other than Christian.[5] The whole community shares in this nurturing Kerygmatic process by intentionally involving the youth in its faith language, its cherished stories, its traditions, its rituals, and its touch. And it is understood that the faith community has a faith bias that shapes those who come in contact with it. But Jones does not stop with *nearness*. He also advocates *directness*. He states:

> . . .There must be specific times when the faith is presented directly to the young person. In some churches, we "beat around the bush" too much. We're often embarrassed in our homes to bring up concerns of faith . . .
>
> Directness occurs when we intentionally aid young persons in writing a new chapter in their faith story. Directness means frank questions and discussions with youth about the meaning of personal faith. Directness includes occasions when worship is intimate, when prayer touches, when service is eye-opening . . . Directness occurs when we share our own faith story and faith bias. . . .[6]

Directness is that other pole of the nurture-conversion argument, but with a sense of appropriateness included. Jones is saying we cannot avoid the implications of the Kerygmatic Proclamation; we should nurture with our faith by being *near* and we should challenge by being *direct*. The worst thing we might be is wishy-washy.

The church, in order to facilitate the journey, needs to be intentional about such nearness and directness. There should be provisions made for on-going groups which are available for a supportive week in and week out exploration of the adolescents' world. Such groups, composed of the youth who travel, some older adults who are willing to enter and re-explore the perimeters of the wilderness and a caring pastor who at times journeys step by step with the band and at other times departs in order that pressing business might be dealt with, are highly intentional "faith shapers" for the journey.

GOD'S "NEVERTHELESS"

Christmas incarnates the presence of God's gift—the presence of the *actual vision* in the midst of all the rough beasts. Christmas is God's "nevertheless" enfleshed in human form. And we are called to such a ministry, a ministry of hope and joy, marked by touch, by nearness and directness, by laughter in the midst of tears. Here, in the Christmas gift of a baby in a manger, we see enfleshed the miracle of love. And, in ministry, we are to become that body, we are to nurture by our nearness and appropriately challenge by our directness.

Let me state it differently: yeast makes bread rise because of the bubbles of gas that it produces. When the yeast is mixed throughout the dough, the bread rises and has the proper airy texture. But if all the yeast is lumped together in one small part of the dough, the bread won't rise evenly and will have big empty holes in it. Even so the church—the loving people gathered— must be intimately and incarnationally involved in life, with people, in the world, in the flour of humanity. When we have clustered ourselves together, fearfully barricaded behind sanctuary walls, we have created great, empty holes in God's world. When we who call ourselves yeast are willing to powerfully love; that is, to become involved in the pain, the despair, and the laughter of life (let's not forget the laughter of life) so that we enable people to grow and become all that they can be, then God's bread will indeed be good to taste because the yeast has penetrated every part of the dough. Being involved with life—intimately mixed through and through it—sounds risky, sounds dangerous, and it is. Yeast dies in the oven, having lost itself to the creation of something new. But this losing of ourselves may well be the only way our own hunger is met.

We are called, individually and collectively, to just such an incarnational ministry as this, to be God's hands, feet, arms, and legs, individually and collectively, in this world. And God remembers, not in flashy neon signs, but in quiet, simple ways as in the baking of bread and as an adult's saying to a young person, "I know you and you are in pain, and I care." We, who were once surprised by a Christmas baby, should expect such tiny, personal glimpses of the incarnate presence of God-with-us. And perhaps, when we are surprised by such glimpses, we will applaud and sing and dance and laugh, for in some mysterious way the *actual vision*, the Christ event, has become enfleshed once more among us. Merry Christmas!

3

Guarantors:
EPIPHANY

A time of Jesus' baptism by John. A time of discipleship, of Jesus issuing his call. A time of ministry, of journey, of reflection on the nature of Christ and discipleship. John Westerhoff speaks of Epiphany:

> On Epiphany we celebrate the story of that blessed journey taken by all those who seek after God's reign. The story we tell is a story of our human journey illumined by the poetry of three wise pilgrims, led by, of all things, a star, through deserts and hazardous unmapped wilds, just to catch a glimpse of a longed-for ruler of earth and heaven . . . These foolish wise folk, these naive,

childlike characters were looking for God's kingdom . . . And they found it by obeying the foolish
wisdom of their imaginations; by acting as if their
dreams were reality; by paying no attention to the
way things really are, and risking a journey in
search of an impossible dream. They let intuition
take precedence over intellect, imagination over
reason. It was a long, mad, lonely journey into a
land some call fantasy land. They were classified as
naive and dismissed by learned and practical folk.

It will always be so when we follow the longings
of our hearts. Those who act upon dreams and
follow stars are rare in an enlightened age. We
prefer to live with certainty. We have difficulty
accepting chaos and surprise. We find it difficult to
give our lives to anything we cannot be sure of.
When we are engrossed in necessary, practical,
everyday affairs, it seems ridiculous to place our
confidence in the unexplainable, to surrender our
lives to what we cannot see, and to live for the
impossible. It appears so foolish, impractical, naive, and irresponsible. . . .

Epiphany is such an invitation to go on a journey
we cannot order or control, following a way we
cannot fully comprehend.[1]

So let us consider the adolescent journey. A journey,
perhaps a ten-year span, from eleven or twelve to the
early twenties. From what to what? A doctor might say
"from not being able to produce babies to being able to
produce and care for children"; a sociologist might say
"the period in which the individual passes from family
life into cultural existence"; a therapist might say "from
being a once powerless and morally submissive child
into being a care-giver and lawyer for the next generation"; a theologian might say "from inheriting a sec-
ondhand faith into owning a faith as one's own."

We know that youth are on journeys which test hope,

will, purpose, competence, love, care, wisdom, and fidelity.[2] Each person's adolescent journey has a payoff: a youth will become either reasonably certain that life makes sense or that it does not. Thus the adolescent journey has to do with the very core of personhood: "to what within me, outside me and of me, can I be faithful, or is there nothing that makes sense, and am I dissolved in apathy?" To be "dissolved in apathy" is to be fragmented and not whole. Many youth dissolve into apathy, do not make it through the adolescent wilderness, and remain trapped in that wilderness without food, maps, and guide. Others pack maps acquired from the culture and employ guides who leave them stranded deep within the wilderness. Still others enter the wilderness searching the sky for beacons; i.e., cults or causes that provide not only maps, but guaranteed routes of travel.

WILDERNESS AND PILGRIMAGE

The wilderness is a land predominantly populated by youthful peers. Among peers in that wilderness is where a significant part of every youth's great adventure takes place, and peer interaction set within specific cultural boundaries provides the arena floor. On this peer floor, in the cultural wilderness, battles are waged: many are bloody, some are caring. The situations played out are a "combination of drivenness and disciplined energy, of irrationality and courageous capability."[3] "Without romanticizing these situations, it can be said that they have the potential for bringing youth closer to the edge of existence, psychologically speaking, than the struggles of any other period."[4] Questions like: "With what peers will I be accepted?" translate into "Will I lose myself?" and "Is there anyone or anything to which I can be faithful?" Erikson suggests that "in no

31

other stage of the life cycle . . . are the promise of finding oneself and the threat of losing oneself so closely allied."[5]

David Ng, in *Youth in the Community of Disciples*, suggests that the word *journey* holds within it elements of human courage and risk while the word *pilgrimage* suggests that identity and faith are divine gifts given during the adolescent search.[6] Whatever term one uses, the youth minister is aware that such a pilgrimage cannot be managed. By this I mean that another one, a greater one (God) has final control, not the youth minister. I recently had a conversation with a youth minister who felt his role in the adolescent pilgrimage was to control all the options available to youth within the church's care. Was there a need for physical play? He sponsored a basketball league and a volleyball league. Was there a need for youth to plan worship? He sponsored a retreat for youth in which all the resources for worship were shared and incorporated by youth. Was there a need for youth to visit colleges? He sponsored a college tour every year for high school juniors. Was there a need to experience mission? He organized several service projects culminating in a work camp. Was there a need for youth music in church? He sponsored youth choirs, including two handbell choirs. One might wonder if all these are truly needs, and one might also wonder at the arrogance of this youth minister's heroic but failed effort to control and to manage the pilgrimage of youth.

The chaos of our world is not so easily controlled or managed. Nor should it be. A part, but only a part, of the role of the one who works with youth is *management*, or administration. I would also argue that *counseling* and *teaching* are minor parts of what an adult in youth ministry does. In my mind the most critical role the adult in youth ministry plays is that of *religious leader* (Chapter 5 on *Easter* deals with ritual leadership in some detail). Unfortunately, youth leaders sometimes manage, teach, and counsel in ways that protect or hide youth from the religious and the *mysterium tremendum* of which we are a part. Again, remembering my comments from Chapters 1 and 2, sometimes we have accepted other visions, languages, and symbols as being more important than the mantle of religious leadership we supposedly incarnate. When we do this, when we manage all the mystery out of life, when we counsel away all the principalities and demons, when we teach fact upon fact, but have dropped the mantle of faith in the mud, then we are but clanging cymbals. Our youth ministry is but a masquerade party sponsored by someone who does not recognize the implications of the Christ story. To quote Westerhoff:

> Each of us . . . has a story. To each community Eucharist we bring our stories and reenact God's story so that God's story and our stories may be made one story. In the context of our liturgies we are initiated into God's story and we appropriate its significance for our lives so that it might influence our common life day by day. And as we journey through history and traverse life-cycle passages, the retelling of God's story sustains us and moves us on.
>   Our most important and fundamental task as Christians is to learn God's story. All our Christian beliefs, experiences, and actions are dependent upon our internalization of God's story, that is, making God's story our story.[7]

The journey has a bigger story. That story frames our pilgrimage, our journey. And we should know, in the story, *whose* we are.

OUR OWN ADOLESCENCE

I start every course on youth ministry I teach with a lengthy process I call "getting in touch with your own

33

adolescence." In that process I ask my students to remember who they were as adolescents and to pick a time and reflect on it through a series of questions about friends, body images, and relationships with important adults. I ask them to recall embarrassing moments as well as moments of great ecstasy. And we process that material in dyads, with the assurance of confidentiality. My hunch is that as adults journey with adolescents our unresolved areas from adolescence will come into play. Did we have difficulty with kids who had more money than we had? Perhaps that insight will help us understand why we get angry today with some kids who seem to have so much. Did we, as adolescents, have difficulty in areas of sexuality or authority? Perhaps insight about those areas will help us when we seem, as adults, to be getting hooked into situations and concerns that sometimes either frighten or anger us. The students usually find this part of the process easy to do, even helpful.

As a part of this class on youth ministry I also ask these fledgling ministers to recapture important images that speak to their spiritual pilgrimage. This is often very, very difficult for them to do. I ask them to reflect on important personal religious stories or metaphors, particularly from the Bible or from important celebrative moments of their lives. Often this is a hard thing; sometimes it is as if not much took place. The pain of this confrontation surfaces in preaching class. "What is your story, your good news?" the instructor asks. "Can you state it in a single line?" Some people do not return; some have instant responses; others wrestle as Jacob did, sweating through long nights.

In all of this my question remains: What are we, as faithing adults, doing when we involve ourselves in *pilgrimage*, in ministry with youth or with anyone, for that matter? And my answer is: we are on a pilgrimage within a particular story and that means certain things.

It means the communion of *koinonia* community; the servant leadership of *diakonia* service; and it means telling the faith story of *kerygma* proclamation. It also means our being a risky and intentional part of the personal and collective incarnation of love within and outside the faithful congregation, that "Body of Christ" as it interacts with the world.

If this is what adults in youth ministry are doing, then the mantle of religious leadership has been picked up and reclaimed. Then, and only then, can we be concerned with administrative tasks, with counseling agendas, and with teaching resources. Then our teaching, our counseling and administrating will be done as part of our greater pilgrimage, a pilgrimage focused by the promised Advent story of one who came at Christmas as a child, but who grew, and who, from Epiphany forward, journeyed *as an adult* in our world.

GUARANTORS

One way to reflect on what Jesus can mean for adults who work with youth in youth ministry is to consider how Jesus was a *guarantor*. A *guarantor* is someone who is appropriately anchored in adulthood but who will walk with youth on their journey. Guarantors share the burden of the journey, help read the road maps and offer encouragement. They incarnate "adultness" in ways that encourage young people to grow. In this way they "guarantee" the fact that adulthood will be a good place to be. A guarantor who stands within the Christian tradition knows that Jesus Christ is the perfect guarantor. By this image Christians understand that the Christ story is the adult story within which I (as a guarantor for youth) can begin to make sense out of how I am to journey with youth. David Ng puts it like this:

35

Jesus Christ is the world's guarantor. "For to this you have been called, because Christ also suffered for you, leaving for an example, that you should follow his steps" (1 Peter 2:21). The Greek word for "example" is *hupogrammos*, the "perfect pattern." In calling Jesus our *hupogrammos*, there is a reference to the primary education of Greek boys, particularly to the way they were taught to write. In those days papyrus was expensive so tablets were used for those who needed to practice writing. These tablets were shadow boxes containing wax. A stylus was used to make the marks, using the pointed end of the stylus for writing and the flat end for smoothing out the wax in order to write on the wax again. The master or teacher would write the words on the tablet which the student copied. The student followed the master's pattern. The master's grooves provided the guidelines. Often the master would take the youngster's hand to guide its strokes. The image in this setting is that learning was not merely a matter of watching some master do an act. What the master did, the student would also do, often with the master doing it along with the pupil. In current terms, learning would involve not merely watching on television as Chris Evert Lloyd hit a tennis ball or listening to the music of Stevie Wonder on a recording. It would be having Lloyd or Wonder do it, then do it with you, to enable you to be able to do it for yourself.

Jesus' own life on earth was a guarantee that our lives can be human and significant too. We learn of life and purpose not merely by the long-distance messages given by God from on high. . . . God says, through Jesus, "Life can be good. This is how to be human. You can do it. This is how. Jesus is our pattern, our guarantor."[8]

Adults who guarantee, who travel with, yet remain adult, who know *whose* they are, who know the story and share the story in faith shaping near and direct

36

ways—such adults are rare, pillars of fire and clouds of smoke in the wilderness, beacons of hope! And we can call such adults guarantors.

Unfortunately, within our culture not many adults sense a call to be guarantors. In *Being Adolescent*, Mihaly Csikszentmihali and Reed Larson report on research that indicates, in terms of sheer amount of time, that peers are by far the greatest presence in an adolescent's life; i.e., very little time is spent in the company of adults. In effect, 1 to 2 percent of an adolescent's time is spent with adults and one might expect the average adolescent to spend one-half hour each week, or five minutes a day, interacting exclusively with their fathers.[9]

So it is that adolescents, both churched and non-churched, move into and through the wilderness, often inadequately armed and yet in hopeful search of guides, beacons, and known pathways. And there are people just slightly ahead of them: some adults who have, in many instances, discovered paths, crossed the rivers bordering the wilderness and stand, apparently triumphant, on the other side. Can that be so? How did they do that? What was it like? Would they become *guarantors* for those now entering the wilderness? In this new role, would they be willing to backtrack and explore alternate routes with these newcomers? Could they serve as helpful leaders and journey on pilgrimage together, as small bands of explorers, sharing maps and food and routes in order that the wilderness not claim yet more victims for the hot sand? Would they respond to a call for discipleship? Will they tell the story?

A MINISTRY OF MEANINGS—JOHN

Ross Snyder's words still stand: "The Church and the public school have a ministry of meanings to perform with young people. Neither can assume that feeding young people with technical reason and with 'what the church believes' is adequate education . . . A ministry of meanings does not exist unless it is also a ministry of relationship. If there is to be communication, or even more importantly 'meeting in the context of creation and redemption,' a 'world' has to be created within which these two people for this length of time, exist."[10]

I know a lay advisor who, for me, is an excellent example of a guarantor involved in such a ministry of meeting. A sixty-year-old who hates committees and anything smacking of bureaucracy, John attends youth gatherings at his local church in order to be in dialogue with youth. John, who knows every youth by name, frequently can be seen engaging a youth in deep conversation. Checking out what he senses might be going on in that young person's world, John often asks direct questions and carefully listens to each response.

Easing newcomers into the youth group is one of John's special priorities. In fact, John serves as a bridge builder between possible youth cliques and the older, adult church community. As one of the church's head ushers, John's usher teams are usually composed of adults and youth. And does the summer intergenerational softball team need an umpire? John volunteers.

One day after church John asked me if I still needed an advisor for a work camp. I did and John said he'd like to come. John came and taught us how to lay shingles, how to drive roofing nails, and how to laugh. John became for that work camp the kind of youth advisor all parents hope their sons and daughters might bump into. At the end of the work camp, John gave everyone a roofing nail.

I'm not sure what others see in roofing nails, but those folk who went on that work camp will never see a roofing nail in exactly the same way again. Now roofing nails sum up an image of John, of John's love, of John's vital faith and his sharing, in communion, a nail for you, and you, and me. John touched all of us with his love.

John is not young nor does he play a guitar. He is not into the careful organization of programs for youth, nor does he attend committee meetings. He has no fancy theory for what youth ministry might be, nor does he orient himself beyond the "now" moment of his intentional dialogues with specific youth. But what John does, and does well, is to actively and intentionally engage youth in caring, confirming, challenging conversations. John cares; when he is at church, he is present for youth. When a church has authentic adults like John engaged in affirmative dialogue with youth, meaning emerges. John is an adult guarantor.

A MINISTRY OF MEANINGS—JUDY

Let's look at a second guarantor, a lay advisor named Judy. Judy, a lay woman both spiritually grounded and caringly aware of the needs of youth within our culture, describes herself in this way:

> I call what I do *"along-side ministry,"* because I know through experience that guidance for youth depends heavily on their own rightful need to determine their own direction. Advocacy with them relies more on a presentation of options and experiences, and I believe my presence with them—an open personal presence—can impact a youth's decisions with criteria which draw on Christian ideals and models.[11]

An adult who believes in an *alongside ministry* with youth, Judy is an example of one who has grown into an understanding of youth ministry as pilgrimage and of herself as a guarantor. Serving with a small group of youth and adults responsible for some facet of the youth ministry program in her local church, Judy pledges time to that group for monthly meetings, talent to that group out of her personal skills, and her all, in the sense of her commitment to the body incarnational image of Christ as an apt metaphor for what that group is all about. She challenges youth about faith; she brings youth near to faith.

She is with them on their pilgrimage in an interesting mix of prayer, business, and social fun. Here youth and adults do all three together. And because there is this framework that encourages relationship and meaning, the team senses that it is a small part of a larger story— the church.

A VOLUNTARY STAFF: ADULTS WITH YOUTH

Central to this model is a voluntary staff; i.e., one or more clusters of youth/adults who are, as an intentional group, responsible in ministry for younger peers. Such clusters, usually composed of several senior high youth church members, two or more adult church guarantors (like John and/or Judy), usually contract among themselves to meet for planning and training in addition to the weekly program meeting for which they serve as staff. What does such a staff look like?

Consider a Presbyterian ninth grade traditionally organized confirmation/commissioning class. Led by the pastor, twelve youth meet weekly from September until Easter in order to explore what *confirming* their vows (taken for them by their parents at each youth's baptism) now means for them. Confirming those vows (in our mythical example), eleven join the Presbyterian Church and are *commissioned* into service but, since this church offers no framework within which youth regularly are encouraged to serve, only one or two wind up teaching in the summer church school program and/or occasionally ushering. The majority drift into silent membership. In Ross Snyder's words: There is no "world" in which a "ministry of meanings" can occur.

That same mythical confirmation/commissioning class, now led by this youth/adult staff, still meets weekly, but is taught by two lay adult advisors (like John and Judy), and three high school juniors and seniors. (1) *Teaching* is only one component on their ministry agenda. This staff is intentional about (2) facilitating *community;* (3) responding with that community in *worship;* and (4) extending that community into *service* beyond the church. Key to this model is a public commissioning of staff members every autumn. In worship each staffer is charged with a fifth responsibility: to *proclaim the good news* to the members of this specific confirmation/commissioning program.

The staff tackles the task of figuring out what happens when *we* meet weekly with twelve ninth graders. Collecting a variety of possible teaching designs, community activities and projects results in a tentatively sketched calendar (including a January retreat and a Maundy Thursday ceremony). Staff meetings become a regular occurrence. While staff agendas vary, each meeting includes time for discussion of: 1) morale and personal hassles; 2) upcoming education designs; 3) long-range plans (like retreats, projects, and designs for worship); and 4) the continual introduction of new ideas related to service, worship, community, teaching, and proclamation. Within such a framework the question of a ministry of meaning with youth begins to make sense.

MINISTRY WITHIN AN OPEN CIRCLE

The form of this youth program is visualized as an open circle. This circle contained no rigid youth/adult hierarchy. When something needed to be done, people, young and old, volunteered and did it. Groups gathered around needs that emerged in ministry. This youth/ adult circle came into being because several adults who had been invited by their pastor to function as youth ministry guarantors with the confirmation class expanded that concept by adding equal amounts of older youth to form a larger leadership team. Within this format youth and adults now plan what will take place. Thus adults minister *with* instead of *to* youth.

If such a youth ministry model is accepted, adults are not included to be in charge of youth, but rather to mutually focus, as member of circle staffs, upon the common tasks facing such staffs. This model strongly affirms the *alongside* ministry style of a Judy. While suggesting that there is much to be done, this model wants to affirm that no one person must do it all. In fact, this model claims that one person doing it to people subverts the idea of church. Pragmatically this means that staff members will be called, for example, to volunteer possible teaching designs. In staff meetings each design will be shared, discussed, and rearranged. In a confirmation/commissioning meeting Judy might then introduce and lead a teaching design that includes a role-play, while two youth staffers might follow her within that same design with responsibilities for discussing the role-play and leading a concluding worship celebration. In that same meeting a fourth staffer might be responsible for promoting the upcoming retreat while John (another adult guarantor) simply listens and participates. Shared team leadership is the hoped-for norm. Thus, effective ministry staffs function as a circle, sharing according to interest and ability.[12]

In our churches, many adults journey with youth in this way. Some adults are regular, always present, fellow and sister travelers; others come and go, yet maintain significant relationships. There are still other unnamed adults in the background, supportive through the larger church, as well as still more representing the extended church family. All these are adults who more or less intentionally share as *guarantors* in the pilgrimage every youth must take.

ON BEING STAR THROWERS

Craig Dykstra suggests that adult guarantors who journey with youth should have the following qualities; they should: "1) enjoy young people and be able to communicate with them; 2) understand the needs and circumstances of youth and be able to provide needed care, support and guidance; 3) know the gospel and communicate it in act and word in relation to the young people's own experience; 4) plan well for and with youth; and 5) have faith and integrity in their lives so that young people can see in them examples of the Christian life."[13] With such guarantors in a ministry of meaning, the story can be told once again in ever new ways. And in this way one generation will lay hands upon another. This is the adult role in youth ministry: to tell the story; to touch as guarantors in caring, faith-shaping ways those who are on a pilgrimage. But we would do well to remember the flip side of such ministry.

Loren Eiseley, a professor of anthropology and the history of science who worked at the University of Pennsylvania, was a poet-scientist who often considered the inhumanity of the inhabitants of this planet Earth. After reading one of Dr. Eiseley's books, W. H. Auden stated he wanted to "read anything of his I could lay my hands on."[14] Auden suggested Eiseley was "a wanderer who is often in danger of being shipwrecked on the shores of Dejection."[15] During one such moment of melancholy, Eiseley found himself lying

43

asleep on a motel bed near the beaches of Costabel. Outside a heavy storm raged and in that pause between night and morning, when dark hesitates, Eiseley went outside. Fires sputtered up and down the beach, and Eiseley knew professional shell collectors were at work. Eiseley was passed by a frantic shell collector who rushed, heavy-laden with starfish, toward a boiling kettle. A second collector, toppling and over-burdened with a huge bag of living shells, whose hidden occupants would soon be consigned to the dissolving waters of the kettles, also pushed past Eiseley. As Eiseley watched, the two men dumped their prizes into the boiling water and stoked the rising fire under their pot. That was the "why" of all the fires on the beach. Shells, once boiled free of all living tissue, could be sold or kept by the most aggressive shell collectors.[16]

Shell collecting seems an apt image for much of what our culture holds as important. Identity is often determined by what a person has or controls. One can imagine shell collectors boiling away, without shame or guilt, the flesh of other humans in order to possess what it is that person owns or has. Certainly liberation theology enters here as one compares first and Third World realities. But shell collectors can also be those folk scrambling up the various high school pyramids.

Everyone builds a faith identity from what has been given and from where their journey has taken them. I, as an adult guarantor work—in tandem with God and the faithful congregation, I believe—in an affirmation of healthy, affirming, caring, whole identities. I like to think that, like Loren Eiseley, I journey through the shell collectors and, moving past them, continue down the beach toward, I hope, a more positive vision.

Intermittent rain squalls, afterthoughts of the storm, scudded by. There was a faint sense of coming light somewhere in the east. As Eiseley rounded a point, the emerging sun pressed red behind him over the shell collectors amid the tumbling blackness of the clouds. And ahead, over a distant point, "a gigantic rainbow of incredible perfection had sprung shimmering into existence. Somewhere toward its foot [Eiseley] saw a human figure standing . . . within the rainbow, though unconscious of his position."[17] Eiseley labored toward that figure over a half mile of uncertain footing. Drawing near, Eiseley saw this man stooping and retrieving a starfish trapped in a pool of silt and sand. Eiseley ventured a comment: "It's still alive." "Yes," the man said, and with a quick yet gentle movement spun the star out into the sea. It sank in a burst of spume, and the waters roared once more. "It may live," he said, "if the offshore pull is strong enough." He spoke gently, and across his bronzed worn face the rainbow light still came and went in subtly altering colors. "There are not many who come this far," Eiseley said. And then, looking at the man, Eiseley asked, "Do you collect?" "Only like this," the man said softly, skipping another star neatly across the water, "and only for the living . . . The stars," he said, "throw well. One can help them. . . ." Eiseley nodded and walked away, leaving him there upon the dune with that great rainbow ranging up the sky behind him.[18]

We can get into the *Star Thrower* image. We toss the kids back into the deep mystery of life, into "yes," toward God. And we prize our victories. Like Rich. Rich was an eighth grader when I first met him, and I, over the years, was there for him. I fancied myself the *Star Thrower*. And Rich grew, went to seminary, became a professional minister. Then, one day, my life fell apart— a six-month separation in my marriage. And I was suddenly empty and afraid. And I, now the star tossed onto the beach with sand in my lungs, I went to Rich and he said, "It's all right, I love you still and yet." And I the *Star Thrower*, became the star, thrown back into the deep.

Star Throwers. Eiseley's image could be said to have

connections with the pilgrimage of Noah as recounted in Genesis. Noah was swept away, flooded, left with no dry earth to stand upon. One day, as the ark bobbed upon the water, a dove returned with a green branch and Noah knew God had not forgotten. As the waters receded, Noah came to stand upon that dry earth. And as Noah responded to God in worship, God set his bow in the sky as a continual sign of relationship. As a promise. As a "yes." Rainbows are of God, open circles, signs of hope for the future, signs of covenant. And we stand—both youth and adults—under and within such circling rainbows. Oh, a rainbow may not always be visible, but it is there. We may be swept away by our culture, by our love of things, by countless issues and problems and yet the rainbow remains. We are known. The rainbow penetrates us and we know *whose* we are. We are known. We stand under and within a rainbow. And the rainbow spills beyond us, cutting deep into the ocean, washing both the thrown star and the thrower in its brilliant color.

Here then is the difference for us who respond to this Exodus tale of Yahweh and a little band of people: youth who travel without such words and symbols, without such images and stories, travel without Yahweh and thus travel with faulty maps. They have no real food and no real guide. They are on journeys that often offer death-worlds instead of life-worlds. The community of faith, the people of God, the church, the keepers of the story of Yahweh and this little band, might consider the implications for living out this story *with* youth, of providing frameworks wherein a staff composed of youth and trusted adults can depthfully explore the meaning of this story as it is played out within their context.

4

The Shadowside: LENT

That time when Jesus was tempted and transfigured. The symbolism of Lent centers on sin, temptation, and penitence. The Lectionary readings include materials from the covenant made in Sinai and the Passion Week, when Christ is crucified, when hope seems lost, when "Yes" seems supplanted by "No."

That great poet of Chicago, Carl Sandburg, once wrote in a poem entitled "Losers":

> If I should pass the tomb of Jonah
> I would stop there and sit for awhile;
> Because I was swallowed one time deep in the
>   dark
> And came out alive after all.[1]

Apparently Sandburg knew what it was like to be "swallowed one time deep in the dark." Possibly, like all poets, he controlled those "swallowed-up places" by creating poetry. Glimpses of Sandburg's swallowed-up place, that deep-in-the-dark place, are embedded in a number of Sandburg's poems. Consider this chilling Sandburg poem about a woman named Maggie:

> I wish to God I never saw you, Mag.
> I wish you never quit your job and came along
> with me.
> I wish we never bought a license and a white
> dress
> For you to get married in the day we ran off to a
> minister
> And told him we would love each other and take
> care of each other
> Always and always long as the sun and the rain
> lasts anywhere.
> Yes, I'm wishing now you lived somewhere away
> from here
> And I was a bum on the bumpers a thousand
> miles away dead broke.
> I wish the kids had never come
> And rent and coal and clothes to pay for
> And a grocery man calling for cash,
> Every day cash for beans and prunes.
> I wish to God I never saw you, Mag.
> I wish to God the kids had never come.[2]

This is a desolate poem. The wish of the man in this poem is to have undone what had once been done. "I wish to God I never saw you, Mag." I wish we had never married. Undo it. But things once done cannot truly be undone, no matter how hard one wishes. And sometimes, because of what we have done, we are desolate, filled with regret, wishing for a second chance, even when we know it is too late. Don't read what I'm saying as a negative statement about divorce. No, I'm speaking of so many acts we do that one day we'd like to undo.

David knew this. One day David saw a very lovely woman bathing. Her name was Bathsheba. David lusted after Bathsheba and wanted her for his wife. There was a bit of a problem because Bathsheba was already married to Uriah, the Hittite, but David had a way of getting what he wanted and getting rid of a husband who stood in his way posed no great problem for him. David's nation was at war, and persons with the courage of Uriah were desperately needed, for Uriah was a great soldier. So David had Uriah sent to the front lines where the fighting was the hottest and the heaviest, and in a few days word came back: "Sir, your servant Uriah has been killed."

The deed had been done. David had succeeded in his evil plan and he could now take Bathsheba as his wife, which he did. But later, when the prophet Nathan told David the pointed story of how a man with only one lamb had that lamb stolen, David knew regret. And then Nathan confronted David by saying: "You are that man," and David wished that what he had done could be undone. It has been suggested that David authored the fifty-first Psalm out of his remorse. If that be so, in that Psalm David puts the deep regret he felt into these words: "For well I know my misdeeds, and my sins confront me all the day long." It is as if David is saying, "Would that I could undo what I have done, but I cannot—what I have done sticks with me." I think David would understand Sandburg's line about being "swallowed one time deep in the dark."

What is it with the Bible anyway? When you really read it, dig into it, you find so many desolate, remorseful, sad stories. Off every page jumps a human who has failed, fallen, been swallowed whole by events so big that seemingly nothing can ever right them. And it's not just the little folk of the Bible who are desolate. No, it's

David and folk like him, the heroes of the Bible. Take a look at Peter, a giant of the New Testament. Early one morning he was standing next to a fire which had been built in a courtyard, when a young girl said of him, "He is one of the Jesus crowd. He was with him." Peter denied it, saying, "I never knew him." Just then, in the distance, a cock crowed and with that sound the terrible thing Peter had done became clear. He remembered the years he had spent with Jesus. He remembered the new and exciting calling into which Jesus had led him. He remembered the hope which had been set afire within him. And now he had denied Jesus. The story of that sad morning ends with these words: "And Peter went away and wept bitterly." Another desolate, remorseful, sad story. Seemingly nothing could ever wipe away such bitter tears. And yet, and yet, it is David who includes in that remorse-filled fifty-first Psalm these lines, "a broken and contrite heart, O God, thou wilt not despise."

Yes, off every page of the Bible jumps a human who has failed, fallen, been swallowed whole, been broken and filled with regret, remorse. And yet, Sandburg's final lines are echoed by these fallen humans: "I was swallowed one time deep in the dark and *came out alive, after all.*" They—David and Peter and so many more— were *swallowed deep and yet came out alive after all.*

What can this mean for you and me, particularly when we consider Lent and youth ministry? We now turn to the shadowside of youth ministry. No one likes to talk about the hassles I raise in this chapter, but the issues they encompass won't go away. They constitute, in some sense, the belly of the whale. The spot Sandburg knew so well.

TOUCH

Many areas could be discussed to illustrate the pervasiveness of the *shadowside*, but let me choose one:

touch. The bad news of today about *touch* between an adult and a youth is that touch is not good, perhaps, in fact, illegal. Let's be honest about this issue. There is cause for concern about touch between adults and youth. I have known a number of adults—male and female—who, in working with youth, have inappropriately stepped over adult/youth lines. One male university student entangled with a seventeen-year-old girl, wound up divorcing his wife. His sociology professor, when told the story, sadly commented, "He worked too closely with the youth culture and joined it." One woman, married, with two young girls of her own, made what I consider inappropriate contact with a male high school senior. The messy situation that occurred was unfortunate for everyone involved in it. And, I should add, my comments are not only based on church adult member activity; I have known several ministers who have sadly mishandled this entire area. There is, unfortunately, much to talk about here—much that is dangerous, both for the adult and the youth involved with the adult. *Touch* is an area in youth ministry that we approach with kid gloves.

And yet, as I mentioned in Chapter 2 on Christmas, the church groups where I felt most at home were groups where touch was a critical ingredient. A high school senior, Mitch, in reflecting upon his experience in one church's youth ministry program where touch was not forbidden made this statement:

> Remember that Tower Hill retreat where we stood in a circle? That was at the end of my ninth grade confirmation class and I remember all year the circle we stood in every Sunday. I remember sitting in that old house in Wisconsin wearing an "I am lovable and capable" sign and asking myself—"Do I want to be part of this?"
>
> Your groups are freaky! . . . I mean, wow . . . that was a new trip for me. And people opened up and talked and cared . . . at church I learned every-

one could help . . . at church I learned—in my gut—about community.[3]

Touch carries a lot of freight with it. In our culture, when a man hugs a man people are amazed. My own father was a deeply sensitive man, yet never greeted me with more than a warm handshake. To hug someone, or to see Michael Douglas, at the 1985 Academy Awards, kiss his father, Kirk Douglas, on the lips, is to be amazed. And yet we need and crave touch.

Those who work intensely with youth have to deal with these kinds of issues on a daily basis. What ground can this adult—this *guarantor*—sense as stable; i.e., what ground can be relied upon? How can someone work through an area like this one? I will share with you one dynamic adopted by me from therapeutic jargon which helps clearly *name* some of the hassles involved in all adult/youth relationships.

YOUTH TRANSFERENCE

I see Daniel walking toward me. His face is set and his emotions hidden. I step in front of him, causing him to face me, and I ask "How was the game?" Without looking me in the eye he mutters, "O.K." and slips by. I ask myself what's going on? Can't he see I'd like to get to know him a little better?

Transference: attitudes dumped on the counselor, therapist, older adult or youth leader *which are transferred to that adult from earlier attitudes and patterns of behavior used with parents and other important persons.* Transference is a kind of repeat performance wherein the counselee interacts or behaves toward the helper (counselor, therapist, youth leader or person in charge) as if that person were someone dredged up from long ago but still important and powerful in the current interaction.

52

Freud initially thought such repeat performances would impede the counseling situation, but he soon realized that transference could be the single most important tool available to the therapist who understood and used it. He noted a negative and positive transference. In fact, positive transference is a counseling hook without which counseling will go nowhere.

Encouraging transference by presenting the therapist as a blank screen upon which the client could project many images worked, but tended to cast the therapist as aloof and in a pulled-back kind of role. Currently, many therapists assume more active roles in the session while still viewing transference as a key tool in therapy. But there are critical differences between *adult* transference and *youth* transference. While the adult, being identified as adult, has some distance from the past in terms of life experience and can look back to a non-adult time as past, a youth has no such distance. Chronologically a youth is still—right now—in the parent/child situation; i.e., most children and youth emotionally remain kids who still exist within primary care groups. Granted, every youth has repressed feelings about parents from the past, and granted, they may react to other adults on the basis of repeating these past patterns, but a youth also acts on the basis of present encounters with primary care givers. Because the adolescent does not so much relive the original trauma as continues to live it, we could say the adolescent is: 1) more invested than an adult in the "right now"; 2) lacking in distance from the parent event; 3) usually, because of closeness, strongly defended and repressed in this area; and 4) lacking sufficient life experience for competently dealing with adults and adult-related issues.

Dealing with transference is even a bigger issue for the younger adolescent (7th, 8th, 9th grades) who is closer to childhood experiences and who deals with the counselor/youth minister as a nearly mirror image of the parent. Younger youth explore the question of transference only in terms of present happenings. Older adolescents (10th, 11th, 12 grades), with identity more secure, have more distance and life experience from which they can recognize and explore connections and alternatives. While adult guarantors can help with this linkage, there always remains the highly present and significant parent(s), so transference is not simply repetition, it is repetition mixed with present event. All adolescent trauma is of this double nature.

Transference occurs not only in one-on-one settings, but also in group settings. In the group this results in a rich, complex underpinning. In particular, the youth minister can be the blank screen upon which everyone unconsciously projects. While a typical youth group is not, per se, a counseling/encounter/T-group, the minister, who is aware of the possible implications of transference and who encourages reality checks coupled with increased personal transparence, will run a healthier group.

COUNTER-TRANSFERENCE

An attractive young girl writes a poem and makes certain Dave, the youth minister, gets to read it:

> How's a kid
> my age
> s'pose to know if she loves
> a guy Dave's age
> the way a kid her age
> is s'pose to . . .
>> (Anne, a high school junior).

The difference between *transference* and *counter-transference* is solely the person about whom the observations and definitions revolve. In *transference* it is the client; in *counter-transference* it is the counselor.

If Dave, taking the poem as an invitation, responds with inappropriate sexual actions toward the young girl, then Dave, with this behavior, is exhibiting *counter-transference*.

Counter-Transference has to do with behavior and feelings in the counselor touched off by a specific client (or behavior and feelings in the youth pastor touched off by a specific youth) and how those feelings are inappropriately handled. While the adult is governed by his or her own psychodynamics, the hook of *counter-transference* is that some unresolved issues in the youth pastor are evoked by a specific youth's behavior. Toward *this* person I have unreasonable likes, dislikes, emotional reactions, dread, pleasure, preoccupations. The point of this description is that Dave's counter-transference toward Anne may result in unaware, unprofessional, and inappropriate behavior. Often such behavior is repetitive, distorts the youth leader's perceptions, and ultimately has an adverse impact on the youth/adult relationship.

In the face of all this, the word *counter-transference* might be said to be a naming of some negative alteration in the behavior of youth pastors; i.e., the pastors are not as effective as they might be because reawakened feelings, instead of helping, are in the way.

DEALING WITH "OUR" ADOLESCENCE

Counter-transference with adolescents is more intense in that the youth leader is re-flooded with adolescent issues. Issues long thought resolved are reawakened by a youth's struggle. Specifically, the areas of sex and authority are frequently unresolved. It is therefore crucial to ask: How does this adolescent touch my issues

55

and reawaken them in ways that make me ineffective? If I indulge in counter-transference, our relationship will become/remain toxic.

What does this mean for those who work with youth? Crucial to working with youth is coming to grips with our own adolescence. I must recognize and learn how to live with the adolescent within me. If I do not recognize and learn to live with my adolescence, the urge to act out repressed authority issues as well as sexual hassles in youth ministry situations can become tragic blind spots.

For example, my father's death occurred while I was in the middle of a counseling relationship with an adolescent named "S". "S" was into a heavy battle with her father; nothing he did was right for "S". She readily verbalized how he tried to boss her around and expressed longing for the day she would leave home. I was aware that "S" did battle with me—quietly yet visibly—in groups. She would subtly put me down with barbed sarcasm and rally others around her as an available alternate "expert." Initially this was quite unnerving to me. Occasionally I would ignore "S" and her barbs; at other times I would fight back. In the two months following my father's death I began to re-evaluate the question of authority, my need to be in control as well as my avoidance of confrontation with those (like "S") who rocked the boat. As this personal evaluation occurred, my relationship with "S" slowly changed. I startled "S" one day when I asked her in what way I reminded her of her father.

The blind spot of my counter-transference was behind us; we would grow toward friendship.

A second example: in my adolescence I kept my sexuality sharply contained. Such repressed adolescent sexuality now seems, for me, to be activated when I work with certain kinds of female adolescents. One such adolescent, "K", caused fantasies to occur within me. Such fantasies seemingly posed attractive possibilities but if I acted out my sexual fantasies with "K", I would be engaging in *counter-transference*. I recognized such behavior as inappropriate and, in addition, highly destructive. Therefore I have found, when working with young women like "K", that I must confront part of my adolescence in an exploration of why I am internally reacting in this particular way.

In both areas—sex and authority—as my blind spots (held over from my adolescence) open up, new ways of interacting are available to me. O.K.; everything I have just said may well be true but there's more to say. The *shadowside* of youth ministry does not end with dynamics like transference and counter-transference; it also has to do with *the messiah complex*, the idea that I can save all these kids!

BEING IN THE BELLY OF THE WHALE

Youth ministers burn out rapidly. Why? One reason is that it's easy to play God. It's easy to program oneself to death. It's easy to accept a church that doesn't co-minister. It's easy to say "I can do it myself." It's hard to say "No." In all of this it's hard to sort out the difference between God's call and your role within that call. Sometimes youth ministers do all the right things; they even understand the dynamics of transference and counter-transference, but things still go wrong. People steal, have unwanted babies, commit suicide. I served with a congregation during the seventies which averaged one suicide per year among youth who in some way were related to our parish. I remember every one of those suicides: one young woman overdosed on drugs; another, also high on drugs, went out a third-floor window and broke her neck; two young men used shotguns; another used a pistol; still another hung himself with his belt. The list continues, but I always found myself saying, "If only I had done something more"; and I sat, alone, in the belly of the whale.

Yet Sandburg suggests that there is, in the Jonah story, the possibility of *transformation*. Indeed, Lent argues that Jesus, who was also sorely tempted, was also transfigured into someone startlingly different. So we, who sometimes find ourselves and at other times put ourselves into the belly of the whale, still have hope. We can come out alive, after all. But how?

COMING OUT ALIVE

When we ask, "How do we get out of the belly of the whale?", God certainly is the key factor we look to to ground an answer; but we must also look to that cluster of frightened people who stood in the shadow of the cross making up their minds about what they should do. And most of them were for heading home. Most of them had been swallowed deep in the dark. Listen to Luke: "We had hoped he was the one to redeem Israel. Yes, and besides all this, it is now the third day since this happened" (Luke 24:21). Catch the unspoken desolation: "We had hoped—oh, how we had hoped! But now, today, Jesus is dead, and we go home; he's been dead three days." The dream was unrealized; they had been swallowed one time deep in the dark, entombed in the tomb of Jonah.

And it wasn't as if these were born winners: Peter was a boaster, a braggart, impetuous; ultimately a coward. James and John were quicker to fight over hoped-for position and status than to understand Jesus' message. Not one seemed to understand what Jesus was about. Again and again he pleads "Can't you see; don't you understand?" Not one stayed awake to be with Jesus, even when he specifically asked. And can you even name them? Oh, sure, Peter, James, John, Thomas—the one who doubted—and Judas, who betrayed him, and . . . well, after that group, the rest seem faceless and nameless. And when some women suggested that Jesus might indeed have risen from the grave, the Bible records, "but these words seemed to them an idle tale, and they did not believe . . ." (Luke 24:11).

But it is surprising! This bunch of losers—yes, losers—this group, "swallowed one time deep in the dark, came out alive, after all." They turned the world upside down. They became (incarnation) the "body of Christ," the Laos (people of God), the church.

Certainly they could not have done this thing alone, by themselves. That's my hunch for those working with youth who encounter the shadowside. My hunch is that everyone is *known* by a God who loves and who stands with us even when we have been swallowed whole. Again and again the Psalmist says, "I was in the pit of despair, and lo, thou art there." My hunch is that I am in a relationship which means that I am not in charge. The "yes" which underlies the universe grounds all ministry; God is in charge. This means: 1) We come out alive when we recognize that *we are not responsible for the world*. God has that job. We are human. We are not the new Messiah. Such kind of care is the wrong kind of care. 2) We come out alive when we not only save time for our friends and family, but *when we plan time with such as these on a regular qualitative basis*. This sixty-and eighty-hour per week business kills friendships and love relationships. When people say with pride that they don't take a day off and have avoided vacations, my response is that even God rested. 3) And we come out alive *when we have a healthy group of peers with whom we play and enjoy the goodness of God's Creation* not only to talk shop, but to enjoy life! I play softball on the pretense of losing weight, but then socialize with the guys over hamburgers after the game! I need this.

59

Yes, we bury ourselves, our best selves. We bury ourselves, but God calls us to ourselves and to grace-filled life. God loves us as we are, yet once touched by God we are transformed into more than what we ever dreamed possible. There is only one of me in the entire world and I have a story to tell. The story is mine alone. But my story is *no* story until I sense how I am known by God—that God loves even me, that God transforms even me, that God, who is the God of Life, stands with me. In spite of my mistakes, my *counter-transferences*, if you will; my "burnt-out places," God still and all and through and through loves me. I am known. Jeremiah put it like this: "Before I formed you in the womb I knew you, and before you were born I consecrated you . . ." (Jeremiah 1:5). As an adult who works with youth, when I know that youth aren't saved by me, then I can let go and live a more fully human life knowing the God of Jacob and Esau, Rebekah and Rachel, stands *with* me. And, like Sandburg,

> If I should pass the tomb of Jonah
> I would stop there and sit for awhile;
> Because I was swallowed one time deep in the
>   dark
> And came out alive after all.

5

Seeing the Kingdom: EASTER

Walter Wink calls Easter "an affront, a riddle and a challenge." He also claims Easter to be "world-transcending." Consider his words:

> No part of the Christian message is more central, ineradicable and *world-transcending* than the resurrection of Jesus, and no part is more difficult to proclaim. It is an *affront* to our world view and our historically conditioned (and constantly changing) notions of what is possible. It is a *riddle* for the historian, defying all explanation. And it is a *challenge* to credulity, since it asserts that God really can be victorious over the injustices and wrongs perpetuated by the powers that be.[1]

Easter. A world-transcending event; an affront and a riddle; and, ultimately, the central challenge for those who work with youth.

THE AFFRONT

Our world view, for the most part, is modern. We have demythologized Easter and feel comfortable with a celebration of that day which is primarily ceremonial. Easter seems to say to a contemporary worshipper that things are OK, will remain OK, and will always be OK even for eternity. Easter, at least as far as our worship experience indicates, is primarily ceremonial, is not concerned about transformation and is usually the logical extension of the dominant modern world view. Easter is a once-a-year validation of our personal masks, our institutional structures and our churchly processes. A casual observer might attend an Easter service of worship and never see or sense anything that could be considered, in Walter Wink's words, to be an "affront."

And yet, ceremony is not always negative in our celebrations. We need ceremony in worship. In the words of my colleague, Robert Moore, ceremony serves to "confirm, consolidate, and legitimate the organization, values, and behaviors of existing structure."[2] Such ceremony in worship is important, even critical, but ceremony in and of itself is not enough for the Christian. Worship, in the world-transcending mode, must be transformative. John Westerhoff puts it like this:

> We have expected too much of nurture. We can nurture persons into institutional religion, but not into mature Christian faith and life. The Christian faith and life by their very natures demand transformations. We do not gradually educate persons by stages to be Christian. To be Christian is to be

baptized into the community of the faithful, but to be mature Christians is to be continually converted and nurtured in the Gospel tradition within a living community of Christian faith.[3]

Here, then, is the Easter *affront*—worship that is more than ceremonial will provide sacred space for the ongoing transformations marking us as an Easter people. We will be seen to be the community of the resurrection and our faith and life, to use Westerhoff's word, will *demand* such transformations, individual and communal.

THE RIDDLE

Walter Wink calls Easter an affront, a riddle, and a challenge. *Riddle* can be defined as "a mystifying, misleading, or puzzling question posed as a problem to be solved or guessed . . . a conundrum, enigma."[4] Our riddle can be stated as a single sentence: "Youth are usually members of this transformed and continually transforming Easter community but they rarely, if ever, participate in worship." How can that be? Arlo Duba, Director of the Chapel at Princeton Seminary, notes the phenomena of seminarians who have never been to church:

> Prior to the 1950's, most church programs involved the whole family for two to three hours of church, with Christian education for all and worship for all. With the increased attendance in the 50's, many churches were forced to two services. With the 60's and 70's this need disappeared, but church after church continues this now unnecessary pattern, with two services, and with the sanctuary less than half filled at each service.

Duba continues:

> The unfortunate and lamentable thing is the con-
> tinuation of the simultaneous worship and Chris-
> tian education programs. In actual practice this
> promotes an assumption, which I hope none of us
> would endorse. It says that the Christian, young or
> old, needs only one or the other, worship *or* Chris-
> tian education. Generally it is education for the
> young and worship for the more mature.

This practice, Duba emphasizes, produces "generation
after generation of young people, including many seminarians, who do not see worship as important to the
Christian life. . . ."[5]

One might protest, as David Ng and Virginia Thomas
do, that children and youth are important members of
the community of faith and should be participants in
the central, transformative, sacred space of that community.[6] But such participation rarely happens. Children and youth should regularly be involved in
worship; instead, well-meaning youth leaders take
youth into the adult worship service once a year for
Youth Sunday. Such Youth Sundays patronize young
Christians precisely because they are convenient ex-
cuses to keep youth out of the regular worship experience.

Not only are Youth Sundays patronizing of youth, but
since they are almost exclusively *thematic*, they almost
always represent worship as an educational object
lesson. While the themes utilized on Youth Sundays are
important, worship doesn't happen that way—at least
transformative worship doesn't. When themes become
a platform for worship, then worship has been triv-
ialized and reduced to a medium for logical explana-
tions. There are no "aha" moments in such worship.
Instead, we sit through a series of "shoulds" and
"oughts."

Kathleen Hughes suggests that our penchant for superimposing themes on worship is the ultimate "manipulation of the Liturgy."[7] Hughes protests:

> We do not celebrate . . . in order to think about ideas, however worthy, but to place ourselves in contact with the person and work of Jesus Christ and to submit to Christ's action in our lives. Liturgy is less a matter of the head than of the heart, an experience less of formation than of transformation, *if* we will let God work the divine will with us.[8]

And there's that word "transformation" again. And what I've described so far—Youth Sundays, "themes" for worship, and one-hour worship ceremonies—hinder transformation and are, at least as I understand worship, antagonistic to the Easter message. Again, Wink claims Easter to be the "world-transcending . . . center of the Christian message;"[9] so, how are we to understand the meaning of our riddle? Here it is again: "If youth are members of the transforming Easter community, why do they rarely, if ever, participate in worship?"

OUR CHALLENGE

By now you can sense where I'm heading. Yes, I am deeply concerned with worship as a core concept of good youth ministry. I am not, however, advocating the "pie slice" theory of youth ministry wherein pie slice "A" is *fun and games,* pie slice "B" is *Bible Study,* pie slice "C" is *social service,* and pie slice "D" is *worship.* That, for me, is a dubious process at best. I think what is needed here is a broader understanding of how worship undergirds all of youth ministry.

Worship permeates youth ministry because youth

ministry has to do with how adults and youth connect within a tradition of faith. In faith traditions believing adults become ritual elders, persons responsible for consecrating and establishing sacred space. As ritual elders they also lift up what it is we are experiencing in dialogue with our ritual symbols, while at the same time maintaining the boundaries of the sacred space.

Consecrating and establishing sacred space in which we dialogue with the holy through ritual symbols in anticipation of transformation is not the same as thematic Youth Sunday ceremonials held once or twice a year. Most Youth Sundays, after all, are spectator sports, much like one-hour TV programs, controlled for show purposes. Most of the participants would be terrified were transformation to erupt during what essentially is a prepackaged program.

Worship in youth ministry is that occasion when sacred space is intentionally sought by ritual elders and, when established, becomes the space wherein life-worlds are challenged and altered, where confessional and celebrational dialogues occur among those gathered and with God inside the warrants and symbols of the Christian faith. I have experienced such moments with youth, most frequently in retreat settings, often on extended trips and occasionally during regularized Sunday morning worship celebrations. The following story illustrates how I think transformative Easter worship is the bedrock of youth ministry:

Tired and sweaty after pedaling sixty miles, a dozen bikers rolled down the last strip of bumpy asphalt into Mackinaw City and The Church of the Straits, our "home away from home." Over supper I became aware of emerging group tensions: some experienced bikers had wanted a one-hundred-mile day, but an inexperienced rider had back pains from a day that, at sixty miles, seemed much too long; three youths felt isolated from the group, while others were anxious to point out what they perceived to be the negative formation of several cliques. Any sense we had of growing community trust was rapidly falling apart. We were experiencing the wilderness.

At this point the celebration of Communion, planned for late that evening, seemed a distant possibility. I had to leave the group with another adult, pick up our second car, and then return, but before I left we held an informal staff meeting. Feelings were aired about cliques, biking distance, the group's lack of cohesiveness, and a growing concern that any time spent away from church that evening would intensify the disunity. Older staff members felt it would be good to have some free time, but that a curfew in preparation for Communion should be set. Everyone met and agreed to postpone Communion until I returned, but if I wasn't back by midnight, everyone would go to bed.

After I left, the fragmented group, quickly tiring of exploring, found itself in the church sanctuary discussing the trip. Things weren't going well. The evening, in the words of one, was "blah." By chance, Ellen, a youth ministry senior staffer who had been the bride in the youth group's mock wedding ceremony three years earlier, discovered a copy of *The Book of Common Worship* in the pulpit. Having served for two years as a confirmation/commissioning youth staff member and sensing this biking group's low morale, Ellen took a chance. Spinning off her training and experience, she involved everyone in a mock funeral followed by a mock wedding. As the role play became elaborate, forays into nursery schoolrooms provided costumes. Seeing in the ritual play a coalescing of the group, the remaining adult adviser, also a staff veteran, encouraged the process while enthusiastically participating.

Twelve-thirty arrived. I was apprehensive as our two vans approached the quiet church. In my mind all the bikers were asleep and Communion would not be held that night. But as I opened the door, I was greeted, not by sleepers or tired youth arguing about sore backs and biking distances, but by a unifed group who applauded my arrival and shouted, "We want Communion!"

Gathered around a clay mug and a loaf of bread, we began our celebration. Thoughts were shared on how everyone yearns for wholeness, for community and for love, and yet finds it hard to risk and reach out. Someone said that in the evening's ritual play; i.e., the funeral and the wedding, the group had buried some of its brokenness and celebrated a coming together in a "wedding" that had included everyone. Confessions were shared. These took an hour and a half and were deeply moving.

After singing several songs, symbols of the week's ride were presented. Frank brought a water bottle, without which he said he would never have survived. To him the water represented life. And we drank his water. Ken brought a bike flag and shared with us his difficulty in keeping up with the rest of his riding group. One time he lagged so far behind his group that he was afraid he was lost. At the next bend in the road he was relieved to see bright orange flags bobbing far ahead directing him on his way. And we touched Ken's bike flag and waved it at one another! I presented my bike's old crank, which had broken on our way to Harbor Springs the day before. I shared with the group about how painful it had been to ride seven miles with a broken crankshaft. I had kept the broken one in my pack as a reminder of what the trip had become for me. And, incredibly, while my broken crank was passed, someone patted my shoulder and read the "Song of Moses" from Deuteronomy 32:10–14, *in passim (Jerusalem Bible):*

> "In the waste land he adopts him,
> in the howling desert of the wilderness.

He protects him, rears him, guards him. . . .
He gives him the heights of the land to ride,
he feeds him on the yield of the mountains, . . .
rich food of the wheat's ear,
and blood of the fermenting grape for drink."[10]

Dick said that Moses' song had grown from experiencing God on that wilderness journey and, like Moses, Dick claimed we also had been protected and guarded, supported and cared for. We had ridden the "heights of the land," eaten "rich food" and shared the "bread" of each other.

Dick continued speaking, saying that we, like bread, were individual grains touched by sun and rain, sweat and toil. We had been at times crushed; at other times bursting with exuberance. Certainly we had been tested by heat and as we had come to know each other we had been redefined, renamed by human hands and mouths. We could see, smell, and hear the cracking of the crust as the bread was broken and passed among us. In tasting it, I recalled the words, "rich food of the wheat's ear." Indeed!

As the wine was passed, Linda reminded us that it, too, like water, alive and flowing, is a symbol of God's presence *with* us. Rich, ripe grapes exploded, squeezed, strained, and fermented into a liquid raised in toasts for joy, this "blood of the fermenting grape" was passed among those who had come to believe that in that room Christ was present.

Then Linda asked us to stand within the sacred space as a circle, and she spoke of pilgrimage and how we were a people with a story, a story marked by both wilderness and promise. God, Linda said, would help us along that wilderness road and, as I looked around the circle into the many pairs of eyes, I realized that in this sacred space I had seen a *marker* in the wilderness, a pillar of fire, a cloud of smoke! In the darkness of that church's basement, bread and a chalice had been shared and our realities had been fractured and altered.

I must confess that I was changed as a result of this experience, for I had entered that moment's sacred space as part of a mixed and hurting collection of individuals, but had left as a member of a tested community. Later that night, as I slipped into my sleeping bag and a deep sleep, I realized that the next day's biking would be a moveable feast. And it was.

PROVOKING SACRED SPACE

While there was an element of serendipity in the bikers' early evening "funeral" and "wedding," there was also a connection for these youth with a long history of worshipping out of shared common experiences as well as an intentional move toward worship by Dick, Linda, and myself. We were the ritual elders, and we took such responsibility seriously. We "provoked" or "established" sacred space by placing powerful symbols—the chalice, the bread, Bible, and candle—in what otherwise would have been an empty room. The presence of those symbols was critical. Also critical was the ready response of the bikers: "We want Communion." This response, merged with the symbols and the intentional ritual leadership, aided in establishing the sacred space.

So it was that in that place the memories of past Communion services, complete with their symbols of brokenness and wholeness, merged with intent into a sacred space where what had been was altered. In that space persons engaged in a suspension of the old patterns: they confessed, cried, embraced. They had fought each other, yet sought clear sight through the common experience of Communion. In a sense, their cry "We want Communion!" rejected the old structures, their cliques, their animosities. It was a cry seeking healing and wholeness. With much pain and with considerable joy they peeled off bits and pieces of the old in anticipation of the new; in a word, they experienced transformation.

TOWARD CLEARER SIGHT

Possibly my favorite poem is by Elizabeth Barrett Browning:

> Earth's crammed with heaven,
> And every common bush
>   afire with God;
> And only he who sees
>   takes off his shoes
> The rest sit round it
>   and pluck blackberries.[11]

When people discuss 10-speed biking with youth groups, some persons concentrate on equipment, routes, safety, and housing; i.e., some people approach biking from a viewpoint that is rational, scientific, logical, and coolly analytical. And we need such thought. When I "see" this way then the "blackberries" are clearly visible; all I need to do is reach out and pick them. Make no mistake, this is the dominant cultural paradigm of our modern time and we build ourselves out of such ways of "seeing." This construction of who we are—coolly scientific and competently measured—works more or less, but those seeking sacred space believe that there are deeper ways of seeing.

An alternative paradigm might suggest every "common bush," every "asphalt road"; indeed, every person "afire with God" if we but have the eyes to see. In such a way of seeing, bikers come to understand bobbing orange flags as directional fires in the wilderness and

71

accept manna as the hand of a helping biker pushing them up a long hill.

Two ways of seeing. But one, the rational, logical, scientific person's way of seeing, is the dominant world view. And yet I, as a Christian, attest to a different way of seeing. I believe that as a ritual elder I have the responsibility to set aside a time and place, to name that space, to provide a container for that moment in which one can move betwixt and between personal and group world views while trying out the new. Such sacred space, set aside with care, where individuals and groups confess and celebrate within the shared symbols of the larger faith pilgrimage in communion with the holy and those gathered inside, such space will provide clear visions of who "I" am, who "we" are and "whose" we are.

What can we point to that will help us in our responsibilities as ritual elders? Certainly it would help to know the tradition, the people, the culture and to be one who believes. That must be said. But we also need to realize that holy ground emerges from our dailiness, not from education lessons or thematic goals. Kathleen Hughes puts it like this:

> Liturgy is not a stepping outside of daily life into some mystical realm but a lifting up of our dailiness, recognizing that we are God-touched yet incomplete. It is a gathering of people who need to let go, to give themselves over, to surrender to the God of Mystery, and to receive grace and strength to keep going.[12]

When I bike with a group, I worship out of what that experience means; when I gather with a group of youth on a Thursday night, I worship out of what that Thursday night means, individually and collectively.

We also need to note that because our lives in our

dailiness are brought to sacred space, the symbols and the anchor bolts (the stories, traditions, etc.) that inform such space need to be present. This shapes the container and provides the boundaries.

TECHNICIANS OF THE SACRED

What I am sharing with you are some of the responsibilities assumed by the youth leader as ritual elder. We're talking about transformative worship here, intentionally named and entered into with the assistance of ritual elders, adults who see the presence of the holy, who can locate sacred space for celebration and profound worship, while at the same time respecting the powerful transformative possibilities of such celebration. My colleague, Robert Moore, has long been concerned about the nature and significance of sacred space in ministry. He claims that while "sacred space cannot be generated by a simple act of will," ritual elders can intentionally help establish, can consecrate the space and can be adequate stewards of its boundaries. He would call such ritual elders "technicians of the sacred."[13]

Consider this: You and I, if we work with youth in youth ministry, are called to be *technicians of the sacred*. We are the ones who are *expected*, and rightly so, to *locate* the holy ground, to help others in the taking off of shoes, even as we recognize where we stand and to appropriately "steward" such transformative space and its boundaries. We are expected to know how to do this; i.e., to understand what this is all about. And this is the bedrock of what youth *ministry* means. Here is where personal and communal world views, values, beliefs, and dispositions will be challenged and altered; here is where transformation occurs.

In such sacred space we who believe will face our

demons and "tolerate the terrors of change with its attendant facing of painful truths and emotions."[14] As Dow Edgerton suggests:

> The old structure is suspended, the new is not yet in place. The person or group has crossed a boundary—not unlike the flight out of Egypt—and inhabits a kind of wilderness. In this wilderness the old structures, both personal and social, no longer apply. The ordered meanings from beyond the crossed boundary are no help. Now order is supplied through the presence of powerful symbols, and the ritual elder who understands their application; now new meanings are shaped and a new future is prepared. Now the boundary is crossed once again, but in a different direction. The movement is into a new situation, not a return to the old. Transformation has occurred. . . . Without the deconstruction of the old structure and status, change does not occur. Old wineskins can't hold new wine.[15]

Or, as Elizabeth Barrett Browning has suggested:

> Earth's crammed with Heaven,
>   And every common bush
>   afire with God;
> And only he who sees
>   takes off his shoes
> The rest sit round it
>   and pluck blackberries.[16]

6

Being the Church: PENTECOST

Easter was a fantastic celebration, but it's over. Reality has inched its way back into the room. The party is finished. The guests pack up and head for home. At Easter Jesus was alive, present, God-with-us-now. And then, all too quickly, Jesus exits a second time, to ascend, and we can't do much except feel lost. Back into the wilderness!

In the aftermath of this experience a group of those who had followed Jesus gathered for the Jewish feast celebrating the wheat harvest. They were talking about what had happened when suddenly, sounding "like the rush of a mighty wind," God appeared to them as "tongues as of fire, distributed and resting on each one of them" (Acts 2:1–3). Can you sense the electricity every person in that room must have known? After this experience they would turn the world upside down. Uncertainty was wiped away with this powerful act of confirmation; now confident, each disciple began to speak with persons from other nations in understandable language about "the mighty works of God" (Acts 2:11).

Pentecost: the birthday of the church—a time alive with new possibilities of community. Pentecost is the actualized promise of a spirit-filled lively faith community. David Ng has perhaps a more realistic assessment (or perhaps more cynical assessment) of today's churches. He states:

> Were we to give a nickel for every example of a redemptive, informed, socially active community of faith supporting a similarly active youth ministry, we could pay for this out of our pocket money and still end up with some change! There are not many programs of youth ministry which are caring, covenanting, ministering communities of faith. In most churches youth ministry is a struggle. Attendance is sporadic. The interests of the young people are elsewhere. The activities are irrelevant in that they neither help the young people to grow nor the church to witness and serve. In some churches the youth program is highly successful in terms of numbers, activities, and fun. These churches run high-powered programs which are planned and conducted by professional youth workers who can provide good food, good singing, ski trips in the winter and river trips in the summer, et cetera, et cetera, et cetera. Yet, after three or four years of either type of youth program, small and struggling or big and eventful, a young person may not have heard the good news that God loves her, that she has an identity and purpose in life, that her sins are forgiven, that she is

called into community, that she has support for her individuality and a place for corporate action and witness. Whole generations of young people will / pass through our youth programs and never hear ╱ the Gospel.[1]

How can Pentecost, the "actualized promise of a spirit-filled, lively faith community" impact youth ministry? How can this occur? No human blueprint can guarantee the presence of the Holy Spirit, but observation of numerous communities leads me to describe an eight-step theological process I believe such groups undergo as they "actualize their promise." (This process is informed by James Poling and Donald E. Miller's book, *Foundations for a Practical Theology of Ministry*.)[2] Here in summary, are the eight steps: 1. Pulse-taking; 2. Naming Our Demons; 3. Cultural Insight; 4. Biblical Imagination; 5. Growing a Design; 6. The Confessional Act; 7. The Community Critique; and 8. The Continued Action.

PULSE-TAKING

A community of people contains within it a rich web of lived experience. We are called to pay attention to this lived experience, to be willing to open ourselves to an exploration of its thick complexity. As Jacob wrestled with God's angel, so we are called to wrestle with meaning. As we do this, we take in complex meanings from the past, find ourselves a place to stand in the present, and stretch toward the future, in hope.

This opening of oneself to lived experience might occur in many ways. To tap into this thick complexity I suggest an intentional probing of the youth. I call such intentionality *pulse-taking*. Pulse-taking can occur in a wide variety of ways: for example, through the simple act of acquiring and processing a list of words—words gathered from the immediate presenting experience of a group, words used to name a group's lived experience.

Let us assume a suicide occurs. The group gathers. One starting point is the naming by the group of words which express where the group locates itself. In this example let us suppose that words like *broken, scared, empty, flooded, hurt, angry,* and *wilderness* emerge. As the words are named and collected, people are invited to share personal stories, concerns, and possibilities around the focal point of one or more of these words. In our example the word "flooded" could emerge as having high priority. The group names their experience "we are flooded." This is pulse-taking from the immediate presenting experience of the group. Such pulse-taking of lived experience can intentionally occur in youth ministry when adult guarantors take time to listen, name, and work through lived experience.

NAMING OUR DEMONS

According to the proposed theological method, we next need to be self-critical; i.e., why are we interested in this whole area and, more specifically, why does a specific word like "flooding" intrigue us? Can this single word become a focus of disciplined exploration by the total community? If the community agrees, we probe deeper. Now we enter the wilderness of uncertainty; here the underlying assumptions of each individual (our "demons") are assessed within the secure context of the community. For example: if the word "flooding" was pulse-chosen because of a recent suicide, the depth question, asked only within the caring arms of community, is "how does this word—flooding—personally and communally connect for us?" What "demons" does it call to life?

Read "demons" as a metaphor and, if the context is secure, all kinds of stuff will emerge: how suicide is an expression of our culture (culture as demon) and "I've" considered it ("my" demon) and how "flooding" happens in school (school as demon) and can drugs help "me" survive (drugs as demon) and does anyone (apathy as demon) care, really? Certainly, in this critical phase, the youth minister/adult guarantor needs to listen and help the conscious and subconscious fears and concerns emerging from this deeper plunge into the pulse-chosen word "flooding."

In all this, the youth minister needs to *share the covenantal aspects* of this issue. Where does God enter into "flooding?" How does God respond to suicide? How can we celebrate the "Yes" of a life if we are flooded? And the youth minister also affirms a confessional stance: "This is what I believe." Poling and Miller suggest that at such a moment the group must make a deliberate decision "to join in a shared exploration of common experiences, practices, interests, issues, dilemmas. This shared exploration includes *a commitment to pursue the truth wherever it may lead,* or in other language, to be open to the spirit of God."[3] *Note well:* This is a commitment, not to a process of fun and games and programs filling space with interesting issues to discuss, but a commitment to a process of disciplined reflection upon our shared (and often scary) life. There is no way a youth minister, or any person, can ultimately control such a process. This is powerful stuff. Transformations are indeed possible—personal, social, international— and can be expected from such a process.

CULTURAL INSIGHTS

If the word "flooding" has been chosen, have I read a newspaper article, heard a poem, listened to a record, or watched a TV program that can help focus what it is like to be flooded now? Perhaps a lay advisor remembers something on suicide from a counseling magazine; some youth is responsible for a resource library and checks out "flood" there; another youth checks the resource shelf in the pastor's study for similar ideas. Cultural insights can be encouraged by a youth leader's pushing into the deeper regions. For example, "flooding and the issue of suicide" could be heavily informed by clinical studies on depression or by commentary from a variety of disciplines. Such cultural perspectives with their particularized languages and metaphors need to be connected within the faith community's tradition and, if the Bible is the part of that tradition being appealed to, then "Biblical imagination" as defined by Walter Bruggemann, can come into play as the complementary part of this ongoing correlation between culture and religion.[4]

BIBLICAL IMAGINATION

Walter Brueggemann encourages us to nurture our historical imagination by becoming *insiders* and therefore *participants* in our covenantal/historical understanding of reality. In doing this, for example, we might creatively imagine what it is to live within the images of the Bible. We ground ourselves when we consider how the Bible is *my* story. *Biblical imagination* might ask in this example if I, today, can relive the flooding image of Noah or if I know what it is like to be a Jonah, trapped in the cold, lonely belly of a whale, separated from God and every human touch. On other occasions, *biblical imagination* might ask: Have I ever experienced forgiveness as Jacob received it from Esau? Is the image of Joseph in the pit looking up at his brothers *my* story?

How does that image feel, taste, and smell for me? Our example of "flooding and the issue of suicide" can be creatively imagined within images from the Bible. The youth minister, if this is the person suggesting the biblical images, would choose and present them *because of their potential to intersect with "cultural insight" and the community's lived experience.* To continue our example: biblical images, drawn in response to the issue of suicide, might include *Jonah and the whale* as well as *Noah and the flood.* If the gathered group wishes to intentionally explore the space where Noah and culture intersects for them, they might intentionally "grow a design."

GROWING A DESIGN

If a youth group has readied itself through (1) pulse-taking and (2) naming its demons while intentionally correlating perspectives from (3) the cultural insights and the images from (4) biblical imagination, then a moment arises out of which (5) a people starts to grow intentional designs for further sharing and exploration within the church. In a previous article I put it like this:

This is "growing a design" time, and a large sack of groceries is being packed with people (pulse-taking and naming our demons), records, school events, books, gameboards, films, group dynamics theory (cultural insights), biblical imagery (biblical imagination), plus prayer and deep commitment.

As the grocery sack is "unpacked" (with the intent to "grow" a meal; i.e., a "design"), things are examined, set side by side. Seeking a balance, something to hold the whole design together—either symmetrically or asymmetrically—the designers manipulate the things that emerge from the sack. Some are discarded, and that

81

trimming may be the hardest thing to do. Something goes into the freezer. A spice startles someone; maybe it offers contrast such as small/large, dark/light. An intrigued staffer relates this spice to a certain experience, story, plan, or happening. Gradually, certain ingredients are arranged in a certain way. An emphasis emerges; a focal point for the design is considered. Newsprint, a blackboard, or a notepad, anchors the tentative design in print. The staff is into something that has grabbed their attention and is pulling them along. No one's taste has been put down and all ideas have been pursued, but people also remind each other that today they are cooking "soup" and *not* "apple pie" (that is tomorrow's job) so a particularly tempting tidbit is set out of reach to be enjoyed tomorrow. Someone adds a pinch of salt and the group relaxes while the sketch, the recipe, the design is read back to the assembled explorers.

Now everyone—not just the two or three initial sketchers—stands once more before the newsprint canvas, considering other youth participants as splashes of color, or darting lines, entering "here" and exiting "there." Will each youth be intrigued, confronted, drawn in by the design's coherence, balance, and rhythm? Will the dab of clown makeup work, and can we actually do the mime we were dreaming for the closure? Perhaps a few things are rearranged, or the initial presentation to the initial explorers sparks a creative response from someone who was outside the initial sketch, and that person adds just the right touch. We stand back and, yes, it seems to hold together! Such *growing of designs* occurs through (1) pulse-taking; (2) naming demons; (3) cultural insight; and (4) biblical imagination. This "design" is rooted uniquely within each particular community, and takes physical expression as (6) a "confessional act."

THE CONFESSIONAL ACT

I understand this to be the *confessional moment* of the process. This is where the design is shared with the larger community (a gathering of peers, the church, a city, the larger world) as an act of faith. Here some members claim this particularity as having importance for their journey. They hold it up to the light of day. They invite participation, reaction, celebration.

Charles Winquist suggests that authentic ministry issues "an invitation to share in a more satisfying vision of what is real and important in our lives."[5] Such ministry, Winquist continues, "draws from tradition and history the symbols and mythological ideas that are necessary for the extension of consciousness in the creation of the spirit."[6] This, then, is the staging of that sharing act, that "extension of consciousness in the creation of the spirit."

Poling and Miller, in speaking of this step, suggest: "There is a moment in all theology when one stands in fear and awe of the depth and mystery of experience. Our rational thought cannot protect us from this moment. It is the existential moment when the community must risk all in order to be faithful to God. It is the moment when we stand before God's direction in our lives. There are greater and lesser degrees of risk, but embedded in every confession is the acknowledgment that one is no longer in control and that one is vulnerable in the presence of an Other that cannot be fully understood. It is at this moment that the community confesses its faith and trusts its life in an elemental way to God."[7]

Such "Confessional Acts" take a variety of forms (worship, confrontation, resourcing, counseling, etc.). What follows is a confessional act grown and led *as an educa-*

tional event by an intergenerational staff for a confirmation class group of younger peers.

Example: Noah as Confessional Act

Let us consider the biblical story of Noah as the starting point of a potent marker in the wilderness. It was
grown by this process. Its root word is "flooding" and
this is one community's staging directions for a confessional statement to be shared with those considering
confirmation of their baptismal vows:

> Entering, people discover a long table covered
> with "people pictures." These pictures have been
> selected from magazines because they capture the
> feeling of being "flooded" or "wiped out." Music
> like Bob Dylan's "A Hard Rain's A 'Gonna Fall" or
> James Taylor's "Fire and Rain" could be playing.
> Ask participants to choose one picture that they
> are intrigued by. When everyone has a picture, the
> group reflects on what *feelings* are contained in the
> "people pictures."
> After the "people pictures" have been shared,
> ask for two volunteers. These two volunteers are,
> nonverbally, to move the entire group into posi-
> tions/expressions that capture the feelings just dis-
> cussed/shared. This "body sculpture" will result in
> people's sitting on the floor, turned out, curled
> up—generally in a pattern of brokenness, aliena-
> tion, and loneliness.
>
> Ask the sculptors to assume positions as part of
> the living sculpture.
>
> Ask people to "get into" what they are feeling,
> explore it, name it deep inside. Give a minute or
> two for this.
>
> With folks still in their positions, tell Noah's
> story: "Have there been times in your life when
> there has been no firm earth to stand on, when the
> bottom has disappeared, when you were flooded,

84

swept away on a vast, chaotic sea, riding the storm out by yourself, totally alone?

"Have you reached out for help and none responded until one day, in a gesture of peace and love, someone came to your little bobbing spot and said, 'I love you?'

"And you knew the promise was real, the waters began to recede; green showed through; life was renewed. Have you lived that moment? Is it an image you can live your life by? It is the simple story of Noah and the flood and the ark and the dove that returned with a promise that the good, green earth would soon be seen again."

Also, and/or read Noah's story—Genesis 6:11–14; 7:1–15, 17–18; 8:3–4, 8–11.

Invite folks to get comfortable but not to move from their spots. Pass out paper and pencils and ask folks to each write about a moment in their lives when they were "flooded."

EXAMPLES: "I got flooded in school; everyone had already gotten into their groups and nobody wanted anyone else; I was truly flooded when I couldn't get into one of the groups."

"When I got suspended from school for drugs, and me and my friend had to talk to the pigs and the principal and it was their word against ours. They didn't take our word."

"The most flooded time of my life was a period of seven months in which I lost my grandmother and my best friend, and three other friends—all through death, which was too final; there is no undoing of it to find each other again."

"Our dog kept running away so we had to get rid of it. I thought with our dog gone it would be the end of the world. And when I saw the truck pull away with my best friend in it, I felt the whole world had turned against me."

Ask folks to share their "flooded moments." If

your group is large, you may wish to break into cluster groups for this sharing period.

You may want to ask whether folks believe that after or with each flood comes a dove with a twig of green hope. Has that been their experience thus far? If so, how has it happened? Have they ever been the twig of green hope for someone in a flood? Discuss.

Closing. If the group members have remained in the sculpture-spots assigned by the two sculptors, fine. Or ask them to re-assume their positions.

Ask one person to play the dove—and to re-sculpt the group from alienation and brokenness to reconciliation and wholeness. One can assume the dove's sculpture will be a circle-form of touching people.

Read Noah's response to God when the water went down; his celebration and God's rainbow.

A short, reflective prayer, "Shalom," and hug— and the design ends.[8]

Commentary on the Example

A coherent design for the confessional act has emerged. All such designs, be they educational or otherwise, once grown, must consider such staging practicalities as who will buy the balloons, lead the discussions, present the closures, and make sure the projectors are ready. But such staging is the power of this approach. A group has owned this process from motivation to the confessional sharing of the design; i.e., if the confirmation staff of our example is composed of five persons, then all five are critically involved in the design's staging.

Such staging has been likened to the traveler's road map or "Trip-Tick"; i.e., a flow chart defining who is responsible for movement and pieces of equipment. In the specific design on "flooding," Ellen and Rich spent considerable time choosing, clipping, and gluing magazine pictures of "flooded people" onto construction paper. Setting up two large tables with these pictures covering the tops, Ellen and Rich also selected music, brought some cookies, and welcomed every participant to this time of exploration with comfortable entry words like "Have a cookie and pick out one picture you can get into." Jackson was the staff member who initiated everyone's gathering into a circle and who helped two persons in the body sculpture sequence. Jackson asked for a non-verbal sculpture and once interjected these words, "OK, let's not talk. It takes away from the sculpture." John is the storyteller on this staff; he told the Noah story at the best moment and did it well. Ellen, Rich, Jackson, and John all circulated after John invited folks to write about flooded moments. The staff had seen this time as the most risky and wanted several people up and around to answer questions and to model serious intentionality. This paid off. The examples came with very little prodding and Jan, one of the lay advisors, gently encouraged sharing, listening, and reflecting upon what such moments were all about. Maintaining the mood, Jackson helped a "dove" resculpt the group, John told the end of the story, including the rainbow, and Jackson closed with prayer and song.

Throughout this process, an observer might note the hidden curriculum of such an approach. Adults and slightly older youth are sharing with slightly younger youth (in a confessional act) a design which provides a framework for getting at important things from both the culture and the traditions of the church.

THE COMMUNITY CRITIQUE

Once the design has been structured and enacted, the community should reflect on how it worked. Does the act carry us forward on our pilgrimage in ways that are (A) developmentally appropriate; (B) liberating here and worldwide; and (C) rich in symbols? Was this design a "marker in the wilderness" or something less? Evaluation can occur immediately following an educational design like "Noah" and then again at the staff meeting that week. Evaluation is helped by occasional comments on participants' 3 × 5 cards.

After this particular design's closure, the staging staff gathered for a moment to check perceptions on what had happened; in this instance all feedback was affirmative: the design could be said to have been a kerygmatic marker in the wilderness for this small band on its pilgrimage.

Because people are powerfully impacted by such designs as they connect within their life worlds, this process functions as a catalyst that encourages a process of awakening bits of cognitive and emotion-laden history from each individual's life world, linking up these bits of personal story under and within the larger story. When this occurs, then the reordering, connecting process targets crucial questions like the following for each participant: "Can I buy into this and own it?" "Can this be *my* story?" "Does it offer something for me and beyond me to which I can be faithful?" "Does this faith image intersect with my life in such a way that offers life-world possibilities for me?" This awakened "whatever it is that I am feeling" emerges as a critique of past, present, and future life-world possibilities within freeing faith images and the wilderness is no longer frightening. A beacon in the wilderness has occurred as a proclamation of a life world in opposition to a death world.

Helping this critiquing process is a group's supportive feedback. Staging should include time when individuals can be asked to intersect with one another's life worlds through song, puppetry, story, dance, media, poetry, and sculpture. Such communication is often one person's effort to symbolize, articulate, describe, and present something he or she now wishes to validate with others. It has been my experience that people who have grown through interaction with such confessional designs seek such moments.

CONTINUED ACTION

If a design of depth has occurred, there will be a cogwheeling pattern of faith imagery and reordered bits and chunks of raw life occurring within and also beyond such a momentary confession by a sharing community. From such an experience there will be a logical and expected continuation into the next day and beyond from what has happened here. This is the eighth step of the method we have been following; i.e., there will be guidelines and specific plans emerging from such correlation and confession into the eighth step: *continued action.*

Because of age, training, and competence the adult leader usually has more educational and facilitative expertise than most of the high school staffers, and it is probable that this person will be seen as the director in the growing of such process designs. However, there will be people within the circle who have better tools in other areas and who will have different power in terms of what they do, or do not do, in a gathering. In any group there might be a writer of poetry, a good interpretive dancer, and a clown workshop leader. So it is that ministry with youth comes together into a unique pattern. Because of this, no two designs will be identical. Ross Snyder has said, "A good design doesn't just happen; you have to work with it. You may have to fracture, shift, re-align shapes. The hardest part may be to simplify the design. Keep thinking. 'Less rather than more.' "9

TRANSFORMATION

To summarize, particular communities relate to the text out of their own setting in ways that assess the relationship more metaphorically than literally. These metaphors cog-wheel with transformational reality, influencing continued action in the world. Poling and Miller suggest their stance when they state:

> We join with those who are calling for a practical theology that is not primarily the science of studying the Bible and developing coherent propositions about God, the world, and appropriate ethical responses, but is directed to the goal of faithful and transforming action by the church in the world. We call for a practical theology that is not primarily a science about faith, but is the development of theological understandings that are appropriate to the ongoing life of particular faith communities. We believe that theological reflection arises when the faithful community tries to relate its current experiences in the world as they are interpreted by cultural metaphors to the tradition of believing communities in the past. Such theological reflection leads to interpretations of the tradition that guide the community in transforming action.[10]

That action might occur *educationally*, as did the example of Noah's flooded moment; or might occur *prophetically*, in the confrontation of some system which promotes suicide; or might occur *pastorally*, in the setting up of a suicide hot-line/prevention center; or might occur as *Liturgy* (the people's response) in the Sunday worship celebration. But, whatever the act, the implication of the model is that of *transformation*.

7

Keeping the Promise:
ALL HALLOWS EVE
AND ALL SAINTS' DAY

Halloween, that night of ghouls and vampires, bats and monsters, a phrase literally meaning "All Hallows Eve," the evening before "All Saints' Day," the day that occurs on November first. Halloween is the night we reserve for moments of terror and things that go bump in the night. But we don't have to wait for Halloween in order to be terrified by monsters.

Consider the *Bloom County* cartoon strip created by Berke Breathed. *Bloom County* is inhabited by folk like Opus, the penguin, Oliver Wendell Jones, the computer hacker, and Binkley, the wise-beyond-his-years little boy who has a closet filled with anxieties. One night, as Binkley sleeps, a giant purple Snorklewacker emerges from his closet and wakes Binkley with these words: "Oh Binkley! Hello! Hello! Your closet of anxieties is again open for your subconscious displeasure!" As Binkley struggles to wake up, the Snorklewacker continues: "Well? What horrors would you like tonight? Monsters? Poltergeists? Dentists? Wait! I know—cockroaches walking on your ceiling!" Binkley asks, "Cockroaches walking on my ceiling?" The giant purple Snorklewacker responds, "*Clumsy* cockroaches walking on your ceiling!" Binkley falls back into his pillow and disdainfully says: "Yeah. Right. I'm terrified." But the Snorklewacker turns to the reader, winks, and pointedly comments: "Guess who sleeps with his mouth open!" And we pity poor Binkley, once more tucked away and dreaming about clumsy cockroaches on the ceiling, even as he sleeps with his mouth open.[1]

While Binkley's anxieties tend to run toward wayward cockroaches and rabid librarians collecting overdue library books, churches considering ministry *with* youth often seem terrified precisely because they believe youth ministry is a closed closet packed with anxieties. And our culture, with its negative hype about youth, doesn't help. If we go with one set of cultural messages, it's easy to put off concerns about adolescence because it's considered to be just a time of innocence and silly fun. But if we go with another set of cultural messages, it's easy to back away from adolescence, because it's a place predominantly populated by scary monsters. Speaking about this problem, Joan Scheff Lipsitz, director of The Center for Early Adolescence, states:

> So we have two extremes in our approach to adolescents, ranging from one of benign neglect to a constant crisis mentality, just as there is a "silly child-dangerous monster" dichotomy in our thoughts about adolescence. Somewhere between these two views of adolescents as innocents and as monsters we need to decide who adolescents

really are and what society's response should be in
providing services for them . . .

[As it is now] we are entangled . . . in stereo-
types so negative that we would find them offen-
sive were they racial, religious, or ethnic. Age-
stereotyping of the young does not offend our sensibilities; it co-opts our sensibilities and blinds us
to the realities of adolescence."[2]

YOUTH AS MONSTERS

"Children as Monsters" summarizes the position of
many American churches prior to 1900. During that
time children were consistently held to be lost in sin,
depraved by nature, and in need of a radical conversion.
It was felt that the only response open to the church was
to convert children at the earliest possible age. The
purpose of the lay-led Sunday School movement was
clear: teach the Bible and out of that teaching convert
sinners. Still, today many youth ministry programs remain anchored in this "youth as monsters" conviction.
Conversion remains the operating dynamic. Such programs are often judged by mainline or more liberal
churches as being misguided and perhaps too con-
servative in their approach to youth ministry. "God-
talk," the memorization of Bible verses, and a high evan-
gelistic component often seem overpowering and ma-
nipulative. Nevertheless, this model of youth ministry
directly raises, in a way the more liberal mainline church
often avoids, the radical claim of the Christ in the lives
of youth.

YOUTH AS INNOCENTS

While the "youth as monster" position is still widely
held by many churches, 1847 saw the writing of *Chris-*

tian Nurture by Horace Bushnell,[3] a book which took as its starting point the contention that youth were innocents. This "youth as innocents" position was the polar opposite of "youth as monsters." Bushnell believed children were born innocent and should be nurtured by parents within a loving and faithful church in order that each child should grow up Christian, never knowing otherwise. The dynamic of this "youth as innocents" position was that good children were to be nurtured, not converted. It has been suggested that Bushnell understood Christianity "not as something that explodes violently within human experience but, rather, as a life into which one grows, even if by fits and starts. The image of God in this vision is less that of one who demands earth-shaking, urgent decisions than as a person who is gentle, accessible, and patient."[4]

PUTTING YOUTH "INTO THE CLOSET"

In the argument between nurture and conversion, between "youth as innocents" and "youth as monsters," most mainline churches embraced innocence and nurture, but not as Bushnell envisioned. During the time Bushnell wrote his book, fifteen-year-olds were still often either totally or semi-independent. In the then still-young republic, one moved rather quickly from being a child to being an adult. "Adolescence" as a word was first proposed in 1904 by G. Stanley Hall to indicate the probable emergence of a new stage of growth in the American context.[5] Largely an invention of Western industrial culture, adolescence, as a stage, described the emerging gap between childhood and adulthood. The persons residing in this gap were judged to be neither children nor adults. What to do with these folk? Those who believed in a Christian nurture approach noted how well the public school controlled and impacted in professional ways those who were now called adolescent. With the founding of The Religious Education Association in 1903 came growing recognition and admiration of professional educators. Mainline congregations built model classrooms, bought age-appropriate progressive curricula, supported the professionalization of Christian educators and provided the necessary organizational frameworks for adult-controlled and nationally designed Youth Fellowships.

In all of these there was a subtle shift in understanding the place of nurture; i.e., the responsibility for nurturing young Christians had moved from the broad societal context of home, community, and church to a more professionally maintained and adult-controlled Church School and Youth Fellowship. Indeed, many churches adopted one-hour-on-Sunday formats where adults worshipped while youth attended Church School classes. The hidden curriculum of such an arrangement was that, while being taught facts about the faith in age-graded isolation, youth were rarely, if ever, involved in the faithful life of the worshipping congregation. Youth, so isolated, therefore lost contact with the "social power" Bushnell assumed would occur within a church community. During these years, youth were "put into the closet" and remained there until the sixties, when many mainline denominations attempted to destroy the once nationally supported youth programs. The official line at that time was that youth should not form separate youth organizations but should be empowered as full members of the congregation. While the national structures were destroyed, in truth few congregations empowered youth. Youth remained "in the closet."

The negative picture which emerged from such a scenario suggested that adolescent members of mainline denominational churches would come to accept the following as being perfectly true:

1) "Worship" is something done only by adults;

2) "Community" means *our* youth group;

3) Christian "education" means the transmission of mostly irrelevant information;

4) "Ministry" is something done only by paid adult professionals;

5) "Conversion," or any radical claim by Christ, is silly nonsense; and,

6) "Nurture" can be understood to be social "fun time" at the church's youth group.

THE NURTURING COMMUNITY

While we are the inheritors of this chain of events, we need not accept it uncritically. Current thought re-visions the *social-nurturing enculturating power* of the faithing community. Michael Warren, commenting on the "nurturing community" suggests that:

> To be effective, ministry with youth must attend to the multiple needs of youth seeking to achieve a balance among many ministries: ministry of the Word, of worship, of guidance and counsel (including education). A brief overview of these ministries reveals how they revolve around the community's own life. The ministry of the Word encompasses all those activities by which the church maintains and proclaims the meanings that bind it together. The ministry of worship is the activity by which a community embodies its understandings and its group life in ritual worship. The ministry of guidance and counsel, including education, embodies those activities by which a community comforts the troubled and shares its wisdom about the human condition. This is a ministry of liberating the human spirit. The ministry of healing involves those activities by which a community follows Jesus' mandate to free the captives, feed the hungry, bind up the wounded, and be a force for justice.

Seen from this angle, youth ministry operates out of the community's life. As a nurturing activity, youth ministry is not content with summoning young people to an intense and warm peer-group fellow-feeling. Important as such intense experiences seem to be for young people, a properly nuanced ministry with youth goes beyond them to pay attention to the distance between much in current culture and the norms of human life set forth in the gospel. When seeking to critique culture, youth ministry is more about challenge than about comfort.[6]

TAPPING THE ROCK

I'm told the oriental character for the word "change" includes the character for the word "risk." *Change* is intertwined with *risk* and, make no mistake, in ministry with youth *the church is called to risk.* But when we risk, we stand in good company. Consider Moses. Moses didn't want any part of God's calling him to lead a rag-tag bunch of Israelites out of Egypt. Moses said, "Take Aaron, not me." But when Moses got into the swing of things he was surprised by what occurred on pilgrimmage with God's people. Moses tapped a rock and water gushed forth; Moses lifted his arms and a dry path appeared and the people walked across. Surprise after surprise!

Usually we don't risk; often we're afraid. We're particularly afraid of ministry with youth. Youth well might be monsters! Or we don't want youth involved in *our* worship. Or (catch the fear) we don't want to engage youth in serious reflection about faith. We'd like to keep youth out of our hair, off in schoolrooms where youth ministry professionals have to cope. Leave youth in the closet and bar the door!

But God makes this claim: we are called as a faith community to actively engage in ministry *with* youth.

Will we hesitatingly tap the rocks we discover as we journey together, seeking fresh water? Will we lightly tap each rock to see if some water trickles forth? Or will we bash and pound on those rocks, confident that we will be surprised by God? My hunch is that on this pilgrimage with youth we will be asked to risk, to risk a great deal, to risk ourselves.

Moses' father-in-law, Jethro, understood this. He saw Moses at the top of the heap and he knew that not only was this not good for Moses, it also wasn't good for the people. If I could paraphrase Jethro's advice to Moses, it might go like this: "Moses, quit trying to run everything; you're going to burn out. You don't need to be king of the hill. There are a lot of folk out there with energy and talent. Share the load." And I love Jethro's final line: "If you do this, and God so commands you, then you will be able to endure, and all the people also will go to their place in peace" (Exodus 18:23).

We tend to forget that we have been raised in a culture that honors competition. As we've come through schools, often we've been taught that helping others isn't called co-operation, it's called cheating. Competition and success and struggle can be good things, but if we forget Jethro's advice, if we, like Moses, try to do it all ourselves, we'll find that when we speak to youth about refreshing water, we'll have parched throats; when we speak to youth about manna in the wilderness, we'll have no bread; and when we cry out to youth: "Peace," "Peace," we'll have no peace.

KISSING THE MONSTER

The delightful children's story entitled *There's a Nightmare in My Closet* begins with a small boy, in bed, facing a closed closet door.[7] He knows there is a monster inside the closet. But when the little boy, trying to be tough, encounters and shoots the monster with a pop-gun, the monster cries! And cries! And the little boy discovers that monsters hurt and have sad places, just like the little boy. And so the little boy invites the monster from the closet to join the little boy in bed, where together they safely fall asleep. Thinking of this enables me to sense the truth of the poet, Rilke's lines:

> How should we be able to forget those ancient myths that are at the beginning of all peoples, the myths about dragons that at the last moment turn into princesses; who are only waiting to see us once beautiful and brave.[8]

A ministry *with* youth which operates out of the community's life brings youth from the artificial closets we have provided for them and affirms their natural God-given talents. It nurtures youth while proclaiming the radical claim of Christ for their lives. This has been the agenda of this book. The church year has served as a gentle framework: *Advent* as a time of promise; *Christmas* as the incarnation of good news; *Epiphany* as the pilgrimage with guarantors who care and confront; *Lent* as the shadow side of ministry; *Easter* as a transforming moment of clear vision; and *Pentecost* as the continual action of a faithful community. Now we consider *All Saints' Day.*

ALL SAINTS' DAY

The Sundays after Pentecost are many, but eventually the green of Pentecost starts to fade; the leaves grow golden and then fall. November is not far away with *Advent promise* close at hand, but not quite yet. First there is *Halloween* with its grinning pumpkins carved to keep death from our door. Halloween, with its witches

99

and goblins, its ghosts and bats, encourages us annually to poke fun at death and dying and all the dragons and monsters of this world. On Halloween we "trick or treat" and fall asleep balanced somewhere between things that go bump in the night and the hope that we will indeed wake up on a day that *overcomes* Halloween. And the next morning, we wake up, still alive, on *All Saints' Day*. We should be clear that *All Saints' Day* celebrates the triumph of those saints who have died in the faith. Receiving its name in the eighth century when the pope began holding special services of worship to honor this "company of saints," *All Saints' Day* celebrates the victory, even in death, of those who have lived in the spirit of Christ. On this day, churches will honor members of their faith community who have died in the past year. These, too, are saints, for *saint* is used in the biblical sense to include anyone who is a faithful believer. You and I are included and so are youth. We are all in this together.

KEEPING THE PROMISE

I grew up in the small town of Oil City, Pennsylvania. Whenever the pastor of our local church wrote a letter to the congregation, it started out: "To All the Saints in Oil City." Saints! You. Me. Grandmothers. Sisters. Brothers. Even Adolescents. Adolescence, for those who believe, is not an in-between-time, a way-stop on the road to "becoming" someone great. Recognize that adolescents are *already* saints, and as saints they ought to be able to affirm their baptismal vows as members of the Body of Christ and get on with ministry. It has been my experience that whenever this occurs youth provide the church's ministry with ample enthusiasm and liveliness. And we should expect nothing less! Perhaps Parker Palmer says it best:

So a community consists not of specialized professionals but of generalized amateurs. It is worth recalling the root meaning of that word "amateur"—it means "lover" or "to love." Love is finally the source of all abundance in life, and it is only when love flows from us that the abundance becomes clear. The key to curing is caring, and it seems more and more obvious that the diseases of our time will be cured not by mere professionals who keep their services scarce, but by an abundance of amateurs who care.[9]

A church filled with amateurs will be about the business of being the Advent promise. Such a church will be more of an open circle and less of a competitive pyramid. The church's cultural agendas will be reflected upon in light of the good news. The gifts of all persons will be honored in the diversity of the people of God. Powerful persons will see, with the clear sight of Easter, the presence of the rainbow, and will respond in celebration and with acts of confession. And when the church fails (as it must) those who are the church will reach back into the depths of their relationship with God, and it will be OK; for with God's help, they will, once again, act to keep the promise. Amen.

Notes

CHAPTER 1

1. Fackre, Gabriel, "Vision of Shalom and Hope of Glory," in *Social Themes of the Christian Year*, Dieter T. Hessel, ed. (Philadelphia: Geneva Press, 1983) p. 32.
2. Bradbury, Ray, *Dandelion Wine* (New York: Bantam; 1975, original: Doubleday, 1957), pp. 9–10. Reprinted by permission of Don Congdon Associates, Inc. Copyright © 1953 by Ray Bradbury; renewed 1981 by Ray Bradbury.
3. Marney, C., *Priests to Each Other* (Valley Forge: Judson Press, 1974).
4. Wolfe, Thomas, *The Right Stuff* (New York: Farrar, Strauss, Giroux, 1979), p. 24. Reprinted by permission of Farrar, Strauss, and Giroux, Inc.
5. Myers, W. R., "Suburbia's High School and the Church," *Religious Education*, Volume LXXII, #3, May–June, 1977, p. 306.
6. Rogers, Carl R., *A Way of Being* (New York: Houghton Mifflin, 1980); Maslow, A. H., *Motivation and Personality* (New York: Harper and Brothers, 1954).

7. Moltmann, H., *The Church in the Power of the Spirit* (New York: Harper and Row, 1975), p. 301.
8. Snyder, Ross, unpublished paper on youth ministry (available from the author at San Anselmo, Calif.), 1975.

CHAPTER 2

1. Auden, W. H., "For the Time Being . . . a Christmas Oratorio," pp. 11–68 in *Religious Drama I: Five Plays* (selected and introduced by Marvin Halversen) (New York: Living Age Books, 1957), pp. 66–67. Reprinted with permission of Macmillan Publishing Company from *Collected Poems* by W. B. Yeats. Copyright 1924 by Macmillan Publishing Company, renewed 1952 by Bertha Georgie Yeats.
2. Finneran, Richard J., ed., *W. B. Yeats: The Poems* (New York: Macmillan Publishing Co., 1983), p. 187.
3. Westerhoff, John, *Will Our Children Have Faith?* (New York: Seabury, 1976), p. 80.
4. Jones, Stephen D., *Faith Shaping* (Valley Forge: Judson Press, 1980), p. 30. Used by permission of Judson Press.
5. Bushnell, Horace, *Christian Nurture* (New Haven: Yale University Press, 1967 (reprinted).
6. Jones, *op. cit.*, p. 32.

CHAPTER 3

1. Westerhoff, John, *A Pilgrim People: Learning Through the Church Year* (Minneapolis, MN: Seabury Press, 1984), pp. 60–61. Copyright © 1984 by John H. Westerhoff III. Reprinted by Harper & Row, Publishers, Inc.
2. Erikson, Erik, *Identity, Youth and Crisis* (New York: W. W. Norton, 1968), pp. 91–142 *in passim*.
3. *Ibid.*, p. 241.
4. Bos, D., *Hypothesis One: The Struggles of Adolescence.* Paper presented at Youth Ministry Symposium, Louisville Theological Seminary, Louisville, Kentucky, 1980.
5. Erikson, *op. cit.*, p. 244.
6. Ng, David, *Youth in the Community of Disciples* (Valley Forge: Judson Press, 1981), pp. 49–50. Used by permission of Judson Press.
7. Westerhoff, *op. cit.*, pp. 1–2.
8. Ng, *op. cit.*, pp. 41–42.
9. Csikszentmihali, Mihaly and Larsen, Reed, *Being Adolescent* (New York: Basic Books, Inc. 1984), p. 73.
10. Snyder, Ross, "A Ministry of Meanings and Relationships," *Pastoral Psychology*, December, 1960, II (109), pp. 18–19.

11. William R. Myers, "Toward a Youth Peer Ministry Model: Ministry With and Not to Youth," pp. 12–16, *New Designs for Youth Development*, Volume 5, September–October, 1984, p. 13.

12. *Ibid.*, pp. 12–16.

13. Dykstra, Craig, paper presented at Youth Ministry Symposium, Louisville Theological Seminary, Louisville, Kentucky, 1980.

14. Auden, W. H., "Introduction: Concerning the Unpredictable," pp. 15–25 from "The Star Thrower," in *The Unexpected Universe* (New York: Harcourt Brace Jovanovich, Inc., 1969), p. 15. Reprinted by permission of Harcourt Brace Jovanovich, Inc.

15. *Ibid.*, p. 19.

16. *Ibid.*, pp. 170–171.

17. *Ibid.* pp. 171–172.

18. *Ibid.* p. 172.

CHAPTER 4

1. Sandburg, Carl, "Losers," *Smoke and Steel* (New York: Harcourt Brace Jovanovich, Inc., 1920; renewed 1948 by Carl Sandburg), p. 13. Reprinted by permission of the publisher.

2. Sandburg, Carl, "Mag," from *Chicago Poems* (New York: Holt, Rinehart and Winston, Inc., 1916; renewed 1944 by Carl Sandburg), p. 189. Reprinted by permission of Harcourt Brace Jovanovich, Inc.

3. As quoted in Myers, W. R., "Suburbia's High School and the Church," *Journal of Religious Education*, Volume LXXII, #3, May–June, 1977, pp. 306–311.

CHAPTER 5

1. Wink, Walter, " 'And the Lord Appeared First to Mary': Sexual Politics in the Resurrection Witness, *in Social Themes of the Christian Year: A Commentary on the Lectionary*, edited by Dieter T. Hessell (Philadelphia: Geneva Press, 1983), p. 177 (emphasis mine). Reprinted and used by permission.

2. Moore, Robert, "Ministry, Sacred Space, and Theological Education: the Legacy of Victor Turner," pp. 87–100 in *Theological Education*, edited by David S. Schuller, The Association of Theological Schools, P.O. Box 130, Vandalia, OH 45377. Autumn, Vol. XXI, No. 1, 1984, p. 93.

3. Westerhoff, John, *Building God's People in a Materialistic Society* (New York: Seabury Press, 1983), p. 52.

4. As found in *Webster's Ninth International Dictionary,* editor in chief, Philip Babcock Gove (Springfield, Mass.: Merriam-Webster, Inc., © 1986, publisher of the Merriam–Webster® Dictionaries. Used by permission.
5. Duba, Arlo, "Seminarians Who Have Never Been to Church," *Monday Morning,* December 3, 1979, pp. 10–11 . . . as quoted in David Ng and Virginia Thomas, *Children in the Worshipping Community* (Atlanta: John Knox Press, 1981), p. 87.
6. Ng and Thomas, *Ibid.*
7. Hughes, Kathleen, "Liturgy, Justice and Peace," pp. 189–202 in *Education for Peace and Justice,* edited by Padraic O'Hare (New York: Harper and Row, 1983), p. 199.
8. *Ibid.,* p. 195.
9. Wink, *op. cit.,* p. 177.
10. From *The Jerusalem Bible.* Reprinted by permission of Doubleday & Company, Inc.
11. Browning, Elizabeth Barrett, "Afire;" *Take Off Your Shoes,* edited by Mark Link, S.J. (U.S.A.: Argus Communications, 1972), p. 105. Public Domain.
12. Hughes, *op. cit.,* p. 192.
13. Moore, Robert L., "Space and Transformation in Human Experience," pp. 126–143 in *Anthropology and the Study of Religion,* edited by Robert L. Moore and Frank E. Reynolds, Center for the Scientific Study of Religion, 5759 S. University Avenue, Chicago, Ill., 60637, p. 136.
14. Moore, "Ministry, Sacred Space, and Theological Education . . ," *op. cit.,* p. 94.
15. Edgerton, Dow, "Worship and Transformation," pp. 11–19, in *The Chicago Theological Seminary Register,* Fall, 1985, Vol. LXXV, #3, p. 14.
16. Browning, *op. cit.,* p. 105.

CHAPTER 6

1. Ng, David, *Youth in the Community of Disciples* (Valley Forge, PA: Judson Press, 1984), pp. 49–59. Used by permission of Judson Press.
2. Poling, James N. and Miller, Donald E. *Foundations for a Practical Theology of Ministry* (Nashville, Abingdon Press, 1985). Used by permission.
3. *Ibid.,* pp. 79–80 (emphasis mine).
4. Brueggemann, W., *The Bible Makes Sense* (Atlanta: John Knox Press, 1977), p. 32.

5. Winquist, Charles, *Practical Hermeneutics* (Chico, CA: Scholars' Press, 1979), p. 41.
6. *Ibid.*, p. 42.
7. Poling and Miller, *op. cit.*, p. 88.
8. Myers, W. R., "10 Designs," in Fletcher, Judy (ed.), *Strategies for Senior Highs, Volume 1*. (Presbyterian Church (USA), Room 1164, 475 Riverside Drive, NY, 1978), pp. 143–145. Used by permission of The Geneva Press.
9. Snyder, Ross, unpublished paper on "Growing a Design" (available from the author at San Anselmo, Calif.), 1973.
10. Poling and Miller, *op. cit.*, p. 26.

CHAPTER 7

1. Breathed, Berke, *'Toons for Our Times: A Bloom County Book of Heavy Meadow Rump 'n Roll* (Boston: Little, Brown and Co., 1984), p. 52. Copyright © 1984 by The Washington Post Company. By permission of Little, Brown and Company.
2. Lipsitz, Joan Scheff, "Adolescent Development: Myths and Realities," reprinted from *Children Today*, Sept.–Oct. 1979.
3. Bushnell, Horace, *Christian Nurture* (New Haven: Yale University Press, 1967 (reprinted).
4. Cherry, Conrad (editor), *Horace Bushnell: Sermons* (New York: Paulist Press, 1985), p. 4.
5. Hall, C. Stanley, *Adolescence: Vol. I* and *Vol. II* (New York: D. Appleton & Co., 1904).
6. Warren, Michael, "Youth and Religious Nurture," pp. 244–256 in *Changing Patterns of Religious Education*, edited by Marvin J. Taylor (Nashville: Abingdon Press, 1984), pp. 252–253. Used by permission.
7. Mayer, Mercer, *There's a Nightmare in My Closet* (New York: Dial Books, 1968).
8. Rilke, Rainer Maria (translated by M. D. Herter), *Letters to a Young Poet* (New York: W. W. Norton & Co., 1984), p. 69.
9. Palmer, Parker, *The Promise of Paradox: A Celebration of Contradictions in the Christian Life* (Notre Dame: Ave Maria Press, 1980), p. 108.